"A fascinating account of Ambassador Kesavapany's remarkable journey from modest origins to a distinguished career in public service and diplomacy – and now, with boundless energy, in community service. Written with his characteristic brevity, wit, charm and candour, it also offers the author's personal glimpse into Singapore's evolution since independence and of his peers and friends who helped shape it."

HE Jawed Ashraf
High Commissioner of India to the Republic of Singapore

"Ambassador Kesavapany has done Singapore a great service by recounting these illuminating and inspiring stories; stories which also provide valuable insights into the history of Singapore (and Malaysia) and into the nature of diplomacy. Personal relationships matter: imagine a Brazilian Ambassador tearing up an EU paper at a WTO meeting just out of solidarity with his friend, Pany. This book will surprise, amuse and entertain you."

Kishore Mahbubani
former Permanent Secretary of the Ministry of Foreign Affairs, Singapore

---

"*From Estate to Embassy: Memories of an Ambassador* is a book full of history and knowledge. It is an invaluable source of guidance and advice for many generations to come.

The author, Mr Kesavapany, is a diplomat, a scholar and an interfaith leader. As Singapore's High Commissioner to many countries as well as Singapore's Permanent Representative to the UN, he represented Singapore to the best of his abilities. His experiences became an asset when he was made the Director of the Institute of Southeast Asian Studies. It was not surprising that our former President SR Nathan was the one who recommended that Kesavapany take up the role of President of the IRO from 2017–2018. It was during Mr Kesavapany's tenure as president that the IRO received its biggest donation (over a quarter million dollars) since its founding in 1949.

I first heard of Kesavapany through Professor Syed Hussein Alatas, the former Head of the Department of Malay Studies (NUS) and Vice-Chancellor (UM), who had very high regard for him and used to say that Kesavapany was highly intelligent and a man of vision. It is no doubt that Mr Kesevapany is an icon that Singapore should be proud of for his tremendous contributions that spanned

Syed Hassan Al-Attas
Imam & Head, Ba'alwie Mosque, Singapore

"I had the good fortune to join, and spend my maiden year at, the Inter-Religious Organisation (IRO), Singapore, during Ambassador Kesavapany's presidency in 2017. Ironically, I had the good fortune to spend my first cycle of reservist duty in the Singapore Armed Forces with the Ambassador's son, Murali, 15 years prior.

Usually armed with a kindness of some sort, a word of encouragement, or a knowing smile, it was immediately clear that Ambassador Kesavapany's many years of leadership in public service and his easy-going personality were twin assets for the IRO.

Ambassador Kesavapany infused in the IRO a renewed energy to drive forward and to urgently reconsider its current standing in a changed world. He introduced and initiated various new programmes during his presidency and supported key modernising initiatives that may very well prove to be fundamental to the future of the IRO's inter-faith work.

True to Ambassador Kesavapany's nature, *From Estate to Embassy* is a modest, elegant and hopeful read about life. I hope others enjoy it as much as I have."

Ben J Benjamin
President, Inter-Religious Organisation, Singapore

"A distinguished diplomat's understated record of a long and dedicated service to his nation."

Ravi Velloor
Associate Editor, *The Straits Times*

"I am delighted that that this long-awaited book, *From Estate to Embassy*, has finally come to surface. But it was worth the wait as it takes time to chronicle in detail the life of an amazing individual. Indeed, Ambassador Kesavapany has led a truly remarkable life in service to nation and community. His contributions are immeasurable and extend beyond his diplomatic service to his indefatigable leadership in the upliftment of the Singapore Indian community and his contributions particularly in the social, inter-faith and charity sectors, all earning him much deserved high admiration and recognition. I can think of no greater honour than to call him my friend."

Ameerali Abdeali, JP, PPA (G), PBM
President, Muslim Kidney Action Association

"Like thirty percent of the graduates of the Malayan Teachers' Training College, Kirkby, Liverpool, (MTTC Kirkby), K Kesavapany (Pany) and I opted out of the teaching profession after serving the government of newly independent Malaya for the contractual period of five years. Pany and I had the same ambition: to become lawyers. However, our financial situation was such that we accepted, gratefully, the offer to be trained as teachers in England.

Pany and I were in the same batch, the fifth, 1955–1957, and in the same English tutorial class under Cambridge graduate, Mr Geofrey Broughton. Pany was his favourite student, topping in the term tests.

There was a spiritual, religious trait in Pany. At Hindu festival times like Deepavali, Kesavapany became the College's Hindu priest. Donned in his Veshti and bare chested, he conducted poojas and recited the mantras with all solemnity and divinity in a shivering cold climate!

At ambassadorial level, Pany was an accomplished diplomat who was known to have worked closely with Minister Mentor Lee Kuan Yew himself. As High Commissioner of Singapore to his native Malaysia, he helped to resolve many a knotty issue between the two countries. It was during that time that Pany organised one of the best attended and most enjoyable Kirkby Reunions in the Concorde Hotel in Kuala Lumpur, patronised by HRH Tuanku Bainun, herself a Kirkbyite of the 1952–1954 batch. Pany was also involved as a principal organiser of the 2018 reunion in Johor Bahru and continues to keep close touch with the Kirkby alumni.

Thank you, Pany, for contributing substantially to the success of the Alumni."

Dato VL Kandan

President, Persatuan Alumni Malayan Teachers' Training College

Kirkby, Liverpool, England

"Kesavapany's skill as a people person able to connect across cultures, sparring with elites and interacting with the man in the street comes through clearly. This book is more than the memoirs of a diplomat. Pany gives us a feel of the societies that he lived in, an insight into the rapid changes in Malaysia and Singapore during his lifetime, as well the challenges facing Singapore as we become a middle aged society."

Ambassador Barry Desker

Distinguished Fellow

S. Rajaratnam School of International Studies, Nanyang Technological University

From ESTATE To EMBASSY

Memories of an Ambassador

K. Kesavapany
with Anitha Devi Pillai

Marshall Cavendish Editions

Published by Marshall Cavendish Editions
An imprint of Marshall Cavendish International

Reprinted 2019, 2020

A member of the
Times Publishing Group

Other Marshall Cavendish Offices
Marshall Cavendish Corporation, 99 White Plains Road, Tarrytown NY 10591-9001, USA • Marshall Cavendish International (Thailand) Co Ltd, 253 Asoke, 12th Flr, Sukhumvit 21 Road, Klongtoey Nua, Wattana, Bangkok 10110, Thailand • Marshall Cavendish (Malaysia) Sdn Bhd, Times Subang, Lot 46, Subang Hi-Tech Industrial Park, Batu Tiga, 40000 Shah Alam, Selangor Darul Ehsan, Malaysia.

National Library Board, Singapore Cataloguing in Publication Data

Name(s): Kesavapany, K. | Pillai, Anitha Devi.
Title: From estate to embassy : memories of an ambassador / K. Kesavapany with Anitha Devi Pillai.
Description: First edition. | Singapore : Marshall Cavendish Editions, [2019]
Identifier(s): OCN 1078777661 | ISBN 978-981-48-4150-4 (paperback)
Subject(s): LCSH: Kesavapany, K. | Ambassadors--Singapore--Biography.
| Diplomats--Singapore--Biography.
Classification: DDC 327.59570092--dc23

Printed in Singapore

Cover photograph by Ashima Suri

I would like to dedicate this book

to my wife Padmini,

my sons Murali and Sashi,

my daughters-in-law Jyoti and Geetha,

and my grandchildren Kishan and Jaynna

for their love and affection.

Contents

Acknowledgements

As can be seen from the story to be unfolded in this book, the late Mr SR Nathan loomed large in my life, starting from the time my wife and I arrived in Singapore to the last days of his life when he performed an act of unforgettable kindness to my family. He was a life-long mentor to me.

The book would not have seen the light of day if not for Dr Anitha Devi Pillai, a lecturer at the National Institute of Education (NIE), Nanyang Technological University. She cajoled and bullied me into completing work on the book. Anitha, I thank you for your selfless labour of love.

I wish to acknowledge Ms Melanie Phua, my teaching assistant at the Singapore Management University, who was with me at the start of the journey. Lawson Law and Sumi Baby Thomas had helped in various stages of the writing of the book.

Mrs Triena Ong, my friend and former colleague at the Institute of Southeast Asian Studies (ISEAS) had also helped with editing the draft. I would like to thank my former ISEAS colleague, Asad Latif, for helping to put the finishing touches to the book. Mr Glenn Wray and Ms Anita Teo, from Marshall Cavendish International (Asia), completed the journey with tender loving care.

On the occasion of my 82nd birthday, I am happy that I am able to celebrate the completion of work on the book and have it launched in 2019.

My heartfelt respects to my in-laws, the Kultars and the Naidus. To my relatives and friends in the globalised village of today, my thanks and gratitude for enriching my journey.

K. Kesavapany
1 March 2019

Foreword

I thank my good friend and old comrade, Ambassador K. Kesavapany (Pany), for giving me the pleasure of contributing the foreword to his memoirs.

Life is a mysterious journey. We cannot choose our parents or the circumstances of our birth. Although we have free will, we often have little or no control over our career or professional life. We definitely have no control over when and how our life is ended.

Pany was born and grew up in a rubber estate in Malaysia. His father was a conductor of the estate. Because of his ability and hard work, he was given the opportunity to study at one of Malaysia's top secondary schools. He applied to be a school teacher and was sent by the Malaysian government to study at Kirkby College, in Liverpool, for two years.

Although Pany was happy teaching, he decided to study for a degree in history at the University of Malaya. His loyal wife, Padmini, worked as a teacher to support him. He graduated with a good degree and applied to join the Malaysian Civil Service. Because of the Bumiputra Policy, he was rejected. Malaysia's loss would be Singapore's gain.

Fate intervened and changed the course of his life and career. He joined the Singapore Civil Service. After spending five years in the Ministry of Labour, he managed to transfer to the Ministry of Foreign Affairs. He found his calling. He became a Singapore Citizen and loved his new career as a Singapore diplomat.

We have worked together twice. The first time was in June 1992. I was appointed to chair the Main Committee at the so-called Earth Summit, in Rio de Janeiro. I had a very good team, consisting of Pany, Chew Tai Soo, Viji Menon, Burhan Gafoor and Richard Grosse from MFA and Khoo Seow Poh and Fong Chee Leong from the Ministry of the Environment. I was successful in my work and will always be grateful to the members of the team.

The second time was in 1996. Pany was our Ambassador to the WTO, in Geneva. He had been elected as the first Chairman of the Council of WTO. Singapore had offered to host the first Ministerial Council. Singapore's offer was accepted by everyone except the United States. The Clinton Administration was angry with Singapore because we had caned an American boy called Michael Fay for vandalism. The then US Trade Representative, Mickey Kantor, was determined to block the offer. Pany decided to put the matter to a vote. Because of Pany's friendship with the US Ambassador, he chose not to follow Kantor's instruction and did that vote. The ministerial meeting was chaired by our then Minister for Trade and Industry, Mr Yeo Cheow Tong. Pany and I worked closely with Mr Yeo and the WTO Secretariat to ensure the success of the meeting.

What makes Pany a successful diplomat?

He is a successful diplomat because he is well read and knowledgeable. He has high EQ and is able to connect with people. He is able to win the friendship and trust of his colleagues. He has the ability to build bridges and to create consensus.

In addition to MFA, Pany has served, with distinction, as the Director of the Yusof Ishak Institute of Southeast Asian Studies. He has reformed and modernised the Singapore Indian Association. He was President of the much-admired Inter-Religious Organisation. He was also a very effective Non-Resident Ambassador to Jordan.

In recent years, Pany and his admirable wife, Padmini, have been helping the poor, the disabled, the marginalized and the needy. In his memoirs, Pany has pleaded for a more systemic and generous approach to helping our poor and our elderly.

On a final note, I would also like to compliment Dr Anitha Devi Pillai for collaborating with Pany on the writing of this book.

Tommy Koh
Professor of Law, NUS
Ambassador-At-Large,
Ministry of Foreign Affairs, Singapore
26 December 2018

A Message

I am most delighted to write this message, not only because Pany is a close friend of many years but also because I see the deeply educative value of this autobiography, which I believe will remind the youth of today that the key to achieving your goals in life are hard work and humility.

Pany's story is a fascinating and easy reading account of how a kampong boy from a rural town in Pahang, Malaya, endeavoured, achieved academic success and made his way up as a teacher, civil servant and then served as one of the most self-effacing diplomats to walk the corridors of power, displaying quiet skills that served Singapore best, at the most critical times in its history. And when all is done, he takes satisfaction in once again being a teacher, imparting his vast experience to those keen on diplomacy and international relations. Yet, despite his elevated roles as mentor and guide, you will read that he always remained a student, and has never stopped learning, including lessons that he has learned from the late President SR Nathan.

The reader will also get to know of Pany's deep interest in the welfare of the man in the street. He makes no bones about his strong views on the rising income inequality and the need for a helping hand to prevent people from falling through the cracks.

This is indeed a book that will inspire the younger generation.

M Bala Subramanion
Centenarian
First Asian Postmaster-General
Singapore

CHAPTER 1

Before the Journey Begins

Of the many memories that will be unfolded in this book is a meeting with Minister Mentor Lee Kuan Yew at the Istana in 2005. After a crucial decision to a matter relating to Malaysia, MM Lee asked me, "Pany, don't you think that the Malaysians now know that the second-generation ministers are calling the shots?"

Looking at him straight in the eye, I replied, "No! The Malaysians still think that you are calling the shots."

Not too pleased with my response, MM Lee hitched up his trousers and paced up and down in the room. However, I felt that he was secretly pleased about still having a role to play in the management of Singapore-Malaysia relations.

How did I come to be where I am today?

Destiny is not created by the shoes we wear but by the steps we take. The journey of my life began in the General Hospital in Kuala Lumpur where I was born on 4 November 1936. My father, Muthial Krishnasamy, was a conductor in an oil palm estate in Glenmarie, about 30 kilometres from Kuala Lumpur. Migrating from Vellore in South India, he arrived in British-administered Malaya in the early 1900s.

As he was English educated, he was able to get an administrative job in the estate. Memories of the first five years of my life in that estate are somewhat hazy. It was only in 1940 when we moved to Kuala Lipis, Pahang, that I began to have a firmer recollection of my life. My father was transferred from Glenmarie Estate to Benta Estate, which was about 60 kilometres from Kuala Lipis, the then capital of the state of Pahang. My family lived amongst a cluster of houses surrounded by coconut trees, which came to be called Toddy Kampong. This was on account of the coconut trees that were tapped for their sap, which was then made into toddy. My siblings and I grew up among Indians, Malays and Chinese, and this was my early introduction to an integrated community. We played cricket and did all the things that the youth of those days used to do, like catching spiders and all other kinds of invented games.

In 1941, the Second World War broke out, and Japanese troops moved into Kuala Lipis. By and large, our family did not have any negative experiences of the Occupation. In fact, as my father and elder brother quickly learned Japanese, they were employed as staff in the Food Control department. This gave them access to staples such as rice, cooking oil and salted fish. My father and brother shared some of these foodstuffs with other people in the kampong, in the spirit of give and take. However, while we had a well-stocked larder, we had no one to cook for us. My mother, Andalammah, who also hailed from India, had a heart attack one morning at the age of 40, and passed away. My father, brothers and I had to fend for ourselves. My family now consisted of my father, my sister, Jayaletchumy, and five boys: Chakrapany, Kothandapany, Thasarathapany, myself and Navaneethapany. My sister had married and moved on to start her own family. So, we had to look after ourselves, with my elder brothers taking on the task of cleaning the house and cooking. A cousin, Jeya, would occasionally drop by to help us with the cooking. My task was to look after the six goats, which provided milk for the family. Any extra milk was bartered with neighbours who grew vegetables. By and large, it was a carefree existence surrounded by family and friends.

This tranquility was disturbed when Chakrapany, in an altercation, slapped a Japanese officer. His only recourse to safety was to run to Singapore, where he joined the Indian National Army (INA). For some time, the Japanese Administration kept our house under surveillance. It was at this time that I first came to hear about the INA and its leader, Netaji Subhas Chandra Bose.

Little did I know that years later I would commission a book on Bose at the suggestion of the late Mr SR Nathan. It was written by Nilanjana Sengupta and entitled *A Gentleman's Word*.[1] It is a comprehensive account of Netaji's legacy and his contribution to India's struggle for freedom. The book was well-received and profiled Nilanjana as a scholar and an informed intellectual.

[1] Nilanjana Sengupta, *A Gentleman's Word: The legacy of Subhas Chandra Bose in Southeast Asia* (Institute of Southeast Asian Studies, 2012).

One fine day when I was six years old, my father brought home a lady and told us that she would be our stepmother. Her name was Subbamah. Twenty years younger than my father, she added four more to the family brood: Govarathnapany, Audiletchumy, Santaletchumy and Lalilaletchumy. Typically, stepmothers are known to breathe fire on their stepchildren, but Subbamah was kind and loving to us. My father was taciturn by nature and we did not, therefore, get to learn much about our Indian roots. This is something I regret until today, as I have not been able to discover my ancestral origins in India.

By the end of the war in 1945, British troops returned to Kuala Lipis. My strongest recollection of this period was the tins of condensed milk and Kraft cheese that the British troops shared with the local children. To this day, these two food items are my favourites, especially the round tins of Kraft cheese, which I could eat a whole tin by myself!

In early 1946, the British Administration restarted the only English school in the town. It was called Clifford School, after Sir Hugh Clifford, who was the Governor of the Straits Settlements and British High Commissioner in Malaya from 1927 to 1930. We were all told to line up according to our ages, and I found myself in the line for Standard One, the equivalent of Primary Three in today's terms. School was largely a pleasant experience, in a multiracial and multicultural setting. The Headmasters were British, while the teachers were Asians, including Indians, Sri Lankans and Burmese. The most notable of the headmasters was Dr GED Lewis, who wrote an excellent book on the geography of Malaysia. It became a textbook in schools, for the study of the subject. The others were Mr Mac Cockendale and Mr GF

Jackson. They were all sports-inclined, and therefore Clifford School acquired a reputation for excellence in sports. I played cricket and rugby, and did long distance running. Among the teachers, the one who made the strongest impression on me was my history teacher, Inche Halimi. His passion for history rubbed off on me and was to stay throughout my life.

Mr Somasundram, Mr Selvanayagam and Mr Sinnappo, all Sri Lankan Tamils, taught English language and English Literature. The grounding in literature that I received from them remains with me. At one time, I could recite lines from the "The Rubáiyát of Omar Khayyám", such as:

> A Book of Verses underneath the Bough,
> A Jug of Wine, A Loaf of Bread – and Thou
> Beside me singing in the Wilderness –
> Oh, Wilderness were Paradise enow!

This early introduction to Sufi literature – a mystical brand of Islam – was again a formative influence in my life. It was to lead me to embrace inter-faith dialogue in later life. Mr Somasundram introduced us to the beauty of English poetry, by poets such as Wordsworth, PB Shelley and Tennyson. The poem "Elegy written in a Country Churchyard" by Thomas Gray was one of the most haunting poems that left a deep impression on me.

Our home in Toddy Kampong was at the back of the Ganesha temple. As such, temple-going was part and parcel of my life. A particular reason for going to the temple was the *prasadam*, the offering made to God and later distributed among the devotees. In 1954, I finished Form Five, and was planning to go to Anderson School in Ipoh for Form Six. The major schools in Malaya then, like Victoria Institution in Kuala Lumpur, Free School in Penang, King George V School in Seremban and King Edward VII in Taiping, accepted students from schools such as mine. While waiting for the term to begin, I took up temporary teaching in Abdullah School, Kuantan, Pahang. I was there for only four months before starting class at Anderson School. When I was moving to Kuantan, my father made a prescient remark. Out of the blue, he said, "It is destined that you will not stay put in one place but move to distant horizons." He added that this had to do with a "chakra wheel" on the sole of my right foot. Alas, he did not live long enough to know how accurate his prediction would be!

When the Cambridge results were released, I found my grades good enough to enter Anderson School as a Form Six Lower student as I had hoped for. Among my classmates was Tunku Razeleigh Hamzah, a prince from the Royal House of Kelantan. He went on to study law, and later became the Finance Minister of Malaysia from 1976 to 1984. History was to show that he would have been "the best Prime Minister that Malaysia never had".[2] Ku Li, as he was popularly called, was the victim of vicissitudes in Malaysian politics of that time. He is still active in the political scene and defended his seat in the 2018 General Elections. We remain friends. Another friend of mine was

[2] http://tommythomas.net/publication-article/the-best-prime-minister-malaysia-never-had-the-edge/

Dr S Selvaratnam, who after studying in the University of Malaya in Singapore, went on to become a World Bank official. We remain in close contact.

The most notable and unforgettable of the teachers at Anderson School was Mr NS Selvamany, who taught me Economics. He was a legend in his time, he was more than a teacher. He was a friend, guide and a source of inspiration. With his prodigious memory, he knew the name of every student who had passed through his hands and kept track of his/her progress in life. Asked why he did this, he would quote the following words of wisdom:

> The water that irrigates the padi field
> also benefits the grass on the bunds.
> I am the grass.

Former Chief Justice Chan Sek Keong and I were privileged to have been "irrigated" by the friendship of this sagacious teacher. CJ Chan was to become one of the best Chief Justices in Singapore's legal history. Describing him as a "first rate world class judicial mind", his successor, Chief Justice Sundaresh Menon, has said, "Chief Justice Chan was almost always the perfect judge to hear a case, any case."

For his lifelong commitment to the teaching profession, Mr Selvamany was bestowed many state awards, but the ones he cherishes most are the ones he received in 1996, Tokoh Guru Perak and in 1997, Tokoh Guru Kebangsaan.

Along with his wife Poovayee, Mr Selvamany continues with his good work of remaining in contact with his students who, on the occasion of his 80th birthday in 2012, published a book called *Selvamany: More Than a Teacher*. The concluding paragraph in the book by the author, Rokiah Talib, sums it all up:[3]

> Cikgu, your contributions and deeds are so enormous as a teacher that if I were an artist I would draw the best portrait of your kindly demeanor; if I were a poet I would pen a beautiful poem to capture and reflect your life's wonderful journey; if I were a composer I would write the best song to sing praises of your good nature; if I were a sculptor I would carve the most handsome statue of your persona. I am but a mere mortal with a limited ability to write, so, it is this book that must represent my utmost gratitude and that of others, as our tribute to you!

As my ambition was to read for law, my subjects were English, History and Economics. However, this was not to be. The result of an application I had made while in Kuantan for a teaching scholarship was announced, and I found myself among one of the 150 who were selected for a two-year course in Kirkby, Liverpool. This was a unique experiment by the Malayan Government to fast-track the training of teachers. It was a prestigious scholarship, and much sought after. So, I set aside my plans to study law and opted for the journey to Britain. Besides, my father had told my siblings and I that he could only afford

[3] Rokiah Talib, *Selvamany: More Than a Teacher* (Penerbit Universiti Kebangsaan Malaysia, 2012) p 273.

to educate us until Form Five. After that, we had to fend for ourselves if we wanted to further our studies.

This training of teachers in the Kirkby programme started in 1951, and 150 trainee teachers were sent to England yearly. It was truly a multiracial, multicultural experience, and we interacted without any inhibitions. As soon as one batch returned, another batch left. Hence, at any one time, there were 300 Malayans in a social setting far away from their homeland. All in all, 1900 teachers graduated from the Kirkby Teachers' Training College.

CHAPTER 2

The Kirkby Experience

The travel from the then Sungei Besi Airport in Kuala Lumpur to Heathrow Airport in the United Kingdom was a trip of a lifetime. We stopped over in six places: first flying from Kuala Lumpur to Rangoon, then to Calcutta, Karachi, Nicosia and Rome, and finally arriving at Heathrow in London.

The journey provided the occasion for the 150 of us to bond and become a cohesive group by the time we reached Kirkby College. Situated in a village six miles from the port city of Liverpool, Kirkby instilled in me the habits of cooperation and co-existence with people of other races. At the same time, we remained mindful of what was going on in our country of birth. An identity of a Malayan nation was being formed at a time when the political leaders were negotiating for independence from the British.

My stay in Kirkby was also an enriching experience intellectually. We had a well-loved principal, Mr GF Gurney, and great teachers. My fellow batchmate, Sarada Menon-Panicker, has described some of them as follows:

I vividly recall
setting foot on English soil
on a chilly autumn morning.

The "do's & dont's" of a new life
in a new land
by the all-powerful **Miss Danielli**
so prim, so proper
a stark reminder of
Ms Courtney of "Mind Your Language" series.

Curfew times
on party nights
had to be adhered to STRICTLY!
God help you and "yours" if you crossed …
Ms Danielli's path
on this golden rule!

Recorder playing at music classes
with hardly a finger moving
was termed "miraculous."
(How "cross" **Mr Cross** got!)
Showers of "blessings" from **Mr Wilson** –
If too close you got!

"Wild" and "Woolly" PE demonstrations –
Followed by encounters with a huge "Polar Bear."
(**Mr Struthers**)

"Desperados" memorising and reproducing
someone else's well-written "Karangan".
(**Cikgu Baharuddin**, too smart for us lah!)

"Oohs!" and "Ahhs!"
from many a lady
when **Dr Fielding**
made an entrance
"Oohs!" and Ahhs!" went on …
Word got around …
one spring
Mrs Fielding showed up!
End of story!

Miss McBain whose well-meaning efforts at match-making
never took off the ground.

Dr Terrett, cruelly nicknamed "Stick Insect" –
was, in fact, delightful!

Mr Naylor's sudden appearance –
To teach us "Natives"
Phonetics
and true, blue Bush House English.

Mr Kennedy, the historian –
With "little lost boy" looks
stirred in tender hearts
motherly instincts.

Mr Jones, from the land of Richard Burton –
Chivalrous, caring, jovial
and a real favourite.

Mr Brian Parker another heart-throb –
He took off for Cyprus
that summer
leaving behind
damsels in distress.

Mr Moorhead a remarkable historian –
His predictions for "Post" Independent MALAYA
gave us food for thought
in "Pre" Independent days.

Miss Gillespie the Infirminarian –
She nursed us through
flues and fevers
and broken bones.
(Broken hearts – NO!)

Then …
There was the day
when "worthy" student counsellors
were to investigate
"The case of the missing cabbages."
The "cabbage thieves"?

None other than
our very own counsellors
(no names Thalha!)
"Papa" **Gurney** outwitted yet again!

There were ...
boisterous block parties.
But **Mr Walker**
from the bonnie-bonnie banks of Loch Lomond
residing in Block One
never seemed to mind!
The open secret was – he was hard of hearing!

The one who made the most impression on me was my English teacher, Mr GF Broughton. He taught me Language Analysis, which was to form a very important ingredient for the later part of my career. He also directed a play, *Noah,* in which I was the main character. My fellow actors were Lee Lye Hock, Patricia Yap and Kamalanathan. Kamalanathan later became a High Court Judge of Malaysia.

Kirkby was perhaps the most carefree period of my entire life. There was no need to bother about meals, as they were all catered for. There was no need to worry about money, because we were given a good allowance, and there was no need to worry about transport, as we all lived in an enclosed compound. The Easter and summer vacations allowed us to make trips to various parts of the UK and the Continent. This was both cheap and easy, as hitchhiking was a popular and safe means of travel then. With friends, I hitchhiked from Land's End to

John O'Groats, the entire British land mass. We travelled to virtually all the countries in Western Europe. Raju Suppiah, Ranjeet Singh, Kamalanathan, Syed Noh and Christopher Lee were among my travelling companions.

One unforgettable escapade was when Raju and I found ourselves locked out of the Youth Hostel we were staying in at a Dutch village. This was because we had passed the hostel's closing hour. As we were wondering what to do, two policemen came to us and asked what we were doing at this time of the night. Upon hearing our story, the policemen took us to the police station where we spent the night. The next morning, after giving us coffee and biscuits, they sent us on our way. This act of kindness of strangers, at unexpected times and in unexpected places, was to lead me in later years to join the Singapore Kindness Movement (SKM) led by my friend, Dr William Wan.

It was in Kirkby that I imbibed the Malayan spirit because Malays, Chinese and Indians were put together in a community setting, devoid of race, language and religious constraints. Kirkby proved to be an enriching experience because of the everlasting friendships that were formed.

Some of these friendships have continued and I keep in touch with many of them. The Kirkby spirit lives in the reunions that are held every two years. The Kirkbyites come for reunions from faraway places like the USA, Canada, Australia and New Zealand. Some of them even make this trip despite physical disabilities. One example is S Raju, my groupmate whose leg was amputated a few months before the Penang reunion in 2014. He got his friend to drive him to Penang and arrived in a wheelchair. Such is the indomitable spirit of Kirkbyites. The latest reunion was held in July 2018 in Johor Bahru. I had the honour of being the lead organiser of the reunion while VL Kandan was the de facto leader.

Some members of the group also came to Singapore where Mrs Umi Nathan (a second batch Kirkbyite) hosted a lunch at the Eurasian Association. In between, groups in various towns meet on their own for lunches and other social occasions. There are also gatherings in places like Perth and Sydney, where a number of Kirkby teachers have settled. In Singapore, a group comprising Sarada Menon-Panicker, Dr Goh Teow Seng, Mary Yeoh Seng Choon, Gnanambikai, Lee Lam Hua, Aw Soh Lin, Mahaya Menon and Jayam Narayanasamy nee Sundram and I get together periodically.

In 2017, VL Kandan, who is now a Dato, was elected the President of the Alumni Society. Taking over from founding president Tan Sri Yahaya, Kandan has made the Kirkby Alumni a vibrant organisation. As a result of the work done by Mohd Thalha and Kandan, a plaque was erected in 2018, on the spot where Kirkby College once stood. The area has since become a housing estate. To record this episode in the history of that area, the Knowsley Town Council has set up a unit in the Town Library to store memorabilia connected to the college. Plans are already being made for a sea cruise in February 2019 and the next reunion in Kuantan in 2020.

The most memorable and defining moment of my two-and-a-half-year stay in Kirkby was the visit by the then Prime Minister of Malaya, Tunku Abdul Rahman, and his entourage. Coming from the negotiations with the British on Malaya's independence, the Tunku came to Kirkby to announce the outcome to the students and to the world. We were the first to know of this game-changing moment for the country. It was indeed an exhilarating moment to hear from the Tunku that an end to British colonialism was drawing near and soon Malayans would be in charge of their destinies. Malaya became independent on 31 August 1957.

Kirkby's continuing relevance in the field of education was recently shown by Tun Siti Hasmah, the wife of Prime Minister Dr Mahathir Mohamad, who called upon Kirkbyites and Brinsfordians,[4] to help arrest the decline of the English language in Malaysia. In her message to the Kirkby alumni in the 2018 *Reunion* souvenir magazine, she said:

> After the Second World War, we would send teacher trainees to Kirkby and Brinsford Lodge. Kirkby closed in 1962 and the last Malaysian left Brinsford Lodge in 1964. So what do we have now?" I said in despair.
>
> We are now in a new dawn with a new Government to revamp the education system. Perhaps we can jump start the tried and tested teaching methods of the fifties. May I suggest that Kirkbyites and

---

[4] Those who had attended Brinsford Lodge, another teacher training college similar to Kirkby in Liverpool.

> Brinsfordians lead in the improvement of the teacher training system, with emphasis on the teaching of good grammatical English. You may be the seventies and eighties, some in the nineties. If Tun Dr Mahathir at 93 can lead in running our beloved nation, you can lead by reviving the teacher training methods of Kirkby and Brinsford Lodge of yester-years.

In following up with Tun Siti Hasmah's message, a group from the Kirkby Alumni is interacting with officials from the Malaysian Ministry of Education to discuss a "Retired English Teachers to Volunteer to be back in Schools" project.

My time in Kirkby ended too soon and my friends and I returned to an independent Malaya to contribute to the moulding of a Merdeka generation of students. The Kirkby years will remain one of the happiest periods of my life.

CHAPTER 3

Once I was a Teacher

In 1958, when reporting for duty at Federal House in Kuala Lumpur, I was told that I had been posted to the Bagan Serai English School, which was sixty kilometres from Taiping, Perak. It was a rural town surrounded by rice fields and oil palm plantations. My main subjects were teaching English Language and English Literature. Amongst the teachers were Mohd Sidek Elamdin, later Dato, who was from the first batch of Kirkbyites, and he was the Deputy Headmaster. A tall and handsome guy who broke many hearts, he found his match in Halimah, a fellow teacher in the school. Sidek went on to have an illustrious career, becoming among other things, Secretary to the Governor of Penang.

Bagan Serai was a small town with nothing much to do except hang out with friends after work hours. I was restless in the small town and asked for a transfer to Penang, where my brother KK Pany worked in the Public Works Department, as this would have brought me closer to my family.

I was posted to Stowell School in Bukit Mertajam, on the mainland. A future Prime Minister of Malaysia, Tun Abdullah Ahmad Badawi, and a Deputy Prime Minister, Datuk Seri Anwar Ibrahim, both hailed from this school. Little did I know that both of them would figure in my life when I became the Singapore High Commissioner to Malaysia in 1997.

I asked for a transfer again, and this time to Georgetown, Penang. I started work at the Westlands Secondary School, which was one of the most notorious schools on the island. Non-performers from the other schools were sent to this school as they were considered "hopeless" cases. As luck would have it, I was made the Discipline Master, in addition to teaching English and Physical Education.

I must have been a very strict Discipline Master because when students were given a choice to see the Headmaster or the Discipline Master, they preferred the former. I am sure I was quite strict but fair because many years later, when I met some of my students, they thanked me for having shaped their lives. One of them was Raju, who became the Chief Fire Officer in Penang. Another student became a Brigadier-General in the Malaysian Armed Forces. One of my students also became a high-flyer in the Malayan Civil Service.

Among the teachers in the school were Mr K Nadarajah, Mr Ahmad Hussein, Mr Emran Khan and Mr Ananthavadivel. They became lifelong friends of mine. Apart from teaching, I undertook social work at the urging of Mr S Vijayaratnam, the State Labour Officer and the President of the Malaysian Hindu Youth Council. Together with a few friends, I helped set up the Hindu Youth Organization (HYO), Penang, and was elected its President. Among the friends who were involved in the setting up of HYO were S Ramachandran,

K Ramoo, Panchacharam and Arulandom. Although religious in name, the orientation of the organisation was social service. Towards this end, we organised the first Deepavali Children's Party in 1960. About 350 children from the Ramakrishna Home, St Nicholas Home, School for the Deaf and Blind, and Poh Liong Kok Children's Home were brought together for fun and games. The Governor of Penang graced the function. Held annually over the past sixty years, it has become an event in the social calendar of the community. Rama, as he is popularly called, was the emcee and the life and soul of the party, with his unforgettable "fan dance". In fact, one year, when it was not held, the children from the Homes rang up Rama and asked why the party was not taking place.

Dato V Sithambaram and his wife, Inbamalar, continue to give their support to this event which brings children of all races together. Dato K Kumarandran also continues to be a staunch supporter.

I have many fond memories of Penang. It was here that I met my wife-to-be, Padmini Palpoo, through Penang HYO. She was then a student at the Penang Teachers Training College. After a brief courtship, we got married in Penang on 26 January 1962. All our friends were very supportive of our marriage and two of them, Vijayratnam and S Sathasivam, the then Registrar of Marriages, were the witnesses to the marriage. Vijayratnam's elder brother, Kumara Kulasingam of Radio Television Malaysia, and his wife Devi, stood staunchly by us. My family instantly welcomed and embraced Padmini. However, her family had some reservations which were overcome with the arrival of our eldest son, Murali, in 1967.

The Hindu Youth Organization was to serve as a platform for social interaction among our friends and several of the interactions ended in marriage, such as with Ramachandran, who married Parvathi.

One year after marriage, in 1963, I visited a friend, Mr Oli Muhammed, in the University of Malaya, Kuala Lumpur. He was Padmini's former college mate and a good friend of mine. I was struck by the beauty of the campus and felt the urge to return to an academic environment. On my return to Penang, I told Padmini that I wanted to study at the university. She was quite shocked, because we had just been married and we had a mountain of debt to settle. Some of her friends were even more shocked and they asked her: "What would happen if he cannot make it? It is a huge risk that you are both taking."

Padmini had faith in me and did not object to my desire to further myself through studies. On the contrary, she supported me with the salary she earned as a teacher. She remained in Penang for a while and joined me a year later. As money was tight, for the trips up and down, I hitched rides on lorries transporting newspapers. It was great fun and Padmini would join me occasionally!

For the final part of my studies, I was granted a bursary by the Sri Mahamariamman Temple in Kuala Lumpur. This help that was given by the temple became embedded in my mind and led me on the path of social service in later years.

On one of my university vacations in 1964, I returned to Penang for a short break. When I heard that Mr Lee Kuan Yew, then Prime Minister of self-governing Singapore, was going to make a speech at a rally in Georgetown Stadium, I decided to attend it. In pouring rain, the crowd stood rapt in attention as Mr Lee unfolded his vision of a Malaysian Malaysia. Among other things, he dreamt, like Martin Luther King, of a nation whose people would live in peace and harmony and enjoy, in equal share, the fruits of the land. This speech left a lasting impression on me, and several years later, it was to serve as the catalyst for a life-changing decision.

CHAPTER 4

Varsity Life

Studying in the beautiful campus at Pantai Valley was a pleasurable experience. I studied History, Economics and Tamil Studies for my first year, and specialised in History in my second and third year. It was here that I first came into contact with Professor Wang Gungwu, who was then a Lecturer in the History Department. Like Mr Halimi in my school in Kuala Lipis, Professor Wang enhanced my interest in the study of history. Little was I to know that our lives would intertwine in later years across the Causeway. Handsome and urbane, he was one of the finest intellectuals I had come across. Professor Ezra F Vogel, Harvard University, has described him as "one of the world's greatest intellectual bridges". Unfortunately, the country of his birth did not appreciate his abilities. He moved to Australia, Hong Kong and finally to Singapore, where he served and continues to serve in many academic institutions, including the Yusof Ishak Institute of Southeast Asian Studies.

Likewise, there was another remarkable teacher, Professor Jan Pluvier, who also inspired me to gravitate towards the study of history. The Dutch national could make history come alive as no one else could.

Among other notable lecturers in the University of Malaya were Professor S Arasaratnam, Professor Khoo Kay Kim, Professor Zanal Abidin, Professor Chandran Mohandas Jeshurun and Professor Jagjit Singh. In the Tamil Studies Department, there were Father Thanninayakam, Professor S Singaravelu and Professor S Devapoobathy.

The late Professor S Arasaratam has left a lasting impression with his research on the history of Indians in the region. His untimely death in his 50s left a void in scholarship pertaining to Southeast Asian history. Although he is no longer with us, his work continues to be widely cited by researchers and historians.

Emeritus Professor Khoo Kay Kim, an expert on Malaysian history, is acknowledged as the "national historian". He served for more than 50 years at the Department of History at the University of Malaya. In 2017, he published a well-written autobiography, *I, KKK: The Autobiography of a Historian*.[5] Padmini and I continue to be in touch with him and his wife, Rathi.

My years at the University of Malaya were a far cry from my time at Kirkby. There was now a heightened degree of political consciousness among the student population. In 1964 to 1966, I was appointed the editor of *Varsity Magazine*, I was also associated with the setting up of the Speakers' Corner in front of the university library. This corner

---

[5] Khoo Kay Kim, *I, KKK: The Autobiography of a Historian* (Kala Publishers, 2017).

became a very popular spot for lunch-time rallies. However, this was a short-lived enterprise as the university closed it down a few years later on account of the heady times the country was facing in the run up to the Merger. This was an indication of the government hardening its attitude to the increasingly strident political activities among the students.

We had all experienced the clamour for Merger that led to the formation of Malaysia in 1963. However, within a short space of three years, this became a clamour for Separation.

As students, we felt that it was better to stay as a united family rather than to break up as separate entities. I was one of those against Separation, and in my capacity as editor of *Varsity Magazine*, I wrote the following in 1963:

> The separation of Malaysia is definitely a retrogressive step. In fact, the geography and history of this region has stressed the point that Singapore is no different from Malaya. We are a land of many races; we are a young nation and aspire to the same ideals and aspirations of a democratic state. Where we do differ is perhaps in our approaches, our economic standards and our political ideals. Why then did Singapore have to separate from Malaysia? The question is as problematic and difficult as the answer to which we seek to obtain.

It could have been the flush of youth but in hindsight, however, it appears that Separation was the best of all possible worlds. Bloodshed was avoided and we did not suffer the fate of many colonies that had slid into anarchy and despotism. On the contrary, both Malaysia and Singapore took separate paths and followed different developmental models to achieve the peace and prosperity that the people in both countries enjoy.

As a sign that this issue has not been put to bed, in September 2018, *The Straits Times* reported that a Singapore historian, Dr Thum Ping Tjin, and his colleagues had approached Malaysian Prime Minister, Dr Mahathir to "take leadership in South-east Asia for the promotion of democracy, human rights, freedom of expression and freedom of information."[6] This was viewed in some quarters as asking Dr Mahathir to interfere in the internal affairs of Singapore. As Member of Parliament, Mr Seah Kian Peng, put it:[7]

> I wonder what deep historical insight prompted him to make this plea, to Dr M, whose views on the Water Agreement with Singapore, and Singapore knowing its place in relation to Malaysia are well-known.

At the time of writing, two other issues have arisen to roil the bilateral relationship: territorial claims and airspace. It remains to be seen how these issues will be resolved.

---

[6] Hazlin Hassan, "Activists invite Malaysia PM Mahathir to conference on democracy" (*The Straits Times*, 30 August 2018) <https://www.straitstimes.com/asia/se-asia/activists-invite-mahathir-to-conference-on-democracy>

[7] "Historian Thum Ping Tjin 'does not wish Singapore well': MP Seah Kian Peng" (Channel NewsAsia, 1 September 2018) <https://www.channelnewsasia.com/news/singapore/historian-thum-ping-tjin-does-not-wish-singapore-well-mp-seah-10675180>

It is worthwhile recollecting what Minister Mentor said in the context of the Pedra Branca dispute in 2009:[8]

> Singapore must remain committed to upholding the rule of the law in the relations between states. If a dispute cannot be resolved by negotiations, it is better to refer to it to a third party dispute settlement mechanism, than allow it to fester and sour bilateral relations.

[8] S Jayakumar & Tommy Koh, *Pedra Branca: The Road to the World Court* (NUS Press, 2009) p xiii.

CHAPTER 5

The Letter from Singapore

After graduating from the University of Malaya with a Second Upper Honours degree, I went back to teaching. The Ministry of Education posted me to the High School, in Klang, a port town about forty kilometres from Kuala Lumpur. I taught History and English Literature to Form Six students. However, my stay in Klang was to be short because my heart was set on the completion of my law degree. I had already passed the external intermediate level University of London LLB exams.

In the meantime, I had applied for two government posts in the Ministry of External Affairs (Wisma Putra) and the Malaysian Civil Service. However, both applications were unsuccessful, as I was told following the interview, that the quota for Malay applicants had not been met.

In October 1967, I received a letter from the Public Service Commission (PSC) in Singapore, inviting me to apply for jobs in the Singapore Civil Service. Apparently, the PSC had obtained a list of names of student graduates from the University of Malaya with good results. They were invited to apply to join the Singapore Civil Service. Two weeks after sending in my application, I received a letter requesting me to come down to Singapore for an interview. Shortly after, I was told that I was successful, and that I could join the Service on 1 November 1967. Following the advice of my friend, Dr Lau Teck Soon, a former teacher who had graduated from Brinsford Lodge,[9] I requested to be posted to the Ministry of Foreign Affairs.

Padmini and I packed our bags and headed to Singapore. Padmini was heavily pregnant with our first child and gave birth to Murali a mere eight days after we arrived in Singapore. People said, "How can you drive such a long distance with your wife so advanced in her pregnancy?"

We persisted as we felt it was better for Murali to be born in Singapore as we had decided to make Singapore our home. We drove at a snail's pace from Kuala Lumpur to Singapore, a journey, with several stops on the way, that took nine hours. The move to a foreign land with no friends or relatives must have been hard on my wife. She never once complained. We set up our first home in Opera Estate, between Siglap and Changi Road. It was a lovely place and remains so today. As Padmini herself put it,[10]

---

[9] A teacher training college for Malaysian students from 1955 to 1964, much like Kirkby in Liverpool.

[10] Anitha Devi Pillai & Puva Arumugam, *From Kerala to Singapore: Voices from the Singapore Malayalee Community* (Marshall Cavendish Editions, 2017) p 162.

It was a difficult period of time for me. Pany was in a new job and I was pregnant and alone. We did not know many people here except Chalu and his wife, Ratha, who was a second cousin to Pany. Murali was born one week after we arrived in Singapore. A gem of a person, Ratha was a pillar of support during the post-delivery period. She remained a close friend and confidant to me till her demise in 2018.

CHAPTER 6

Working in the Ministry of Labour

On the first day, I reported to the Public Service Commission (PSC), which was then at the Fullerton Building, fully expecting to be posted to the Ministry of Foreign Affairs. To my utter disappointment, the officer who dealt with my posting told me that I was assigned to the Ministry of Labour.

Taken aback, I asked for the reason for the change in my posting. I was told that Mr Pang Tee Pow, who was then the Permanent Secretary of the Ministry of Labour, had demanded that the next Administrative Service Officer who was recruited by PSC be sent to his Ministry. Mr Pang was a powerful figure in the Administrative Service and no one dared trifle with his demand.

So off I went to the Ministry of Labour on 3 November 1967 and reported for duty at the Labour Court. This was a special court within the Ministry of Labour to address minor labour disputes, mainly through counselling and mediation.

It was a rather unique experience to sit as a "judge" and have lawyers appear before me to plead their clients' cases. Very soon, I was joined by Lee Shuang Hui and Wong Kan Seng, and we became fast friends.

Kan Seng was to rise rapidly up the ladder and ended his political career as Deputy Prime Minister. I was a witness at his wedding to Hong Geok. However high he rose in rank, Kan Seng never forgot the start of our relationship and he would always introduce me to his friends as the person who had been the witness to his marriage.

In 1968, Wong Hung Khim joined us as the Principal Assistant Secretary in the Ministry. He, too, went on to have an illustrious career in the Civil Service. Highly accomplished and with good PR skills, he became the Permanent Secretary in several ministries and headed several statutory boards.

Mr S Rajaratnam, one of the core first generation leaders, handled both the Ministry of Foreign Affairs and Ministry of Labour portfolios. It was during his term that the Labour, Industrial Relations, and Arbitration Court Acts were passed by Parliament.

These laws, described as "draconian" by some quarters, ushered in a period of industrial peace and stability, which in turn set the stage for Singapore's rapid economic progress.

In retrospect, it was a blessing in disguise to have spent five years from 1967 to 1972 in the Ministry of Labour because I came to experience, firsthand, some of the most pressing labour and industrial relations problems that Singapore was facing. Strikes were an everyday occurrence and the trade unions were split into pro-government and anti-government camps. Unemployment was at an unprecedented rate of 14%.

Situated in the heart of Chinatown, the Ministry of Labour was faced with frequent demonstrations by left-wing unions. At times, it was not even safe to venture out for lunch.

If not for the harsh laws, Singapore would not have enjoyed industrial peace and attracted the attention of foreign investors, particularly multi-national corporations (MNCs). The prevailing developmental theology among Third World countries was to shun MNCs as they were viewed as "agents of exploitation". Singapore took a contrary view and welcomed the MNCs. This was because they had technical knowledge, capital and markets, all three factors of production which Singapore did not have. The first MNC to come to Singapore was Texas Instruments. Within sixty days of starting operations, the company was able to send Singapore-produced microchips back to the US. This was the start of the Information Technology (IT) industry in Singapore.

It was at this time, 1968 to be precise, that the British dropped their bombshell of evacuation from their military bases in Singapore, under the "East of Suez" policy. With the loss of empire and a worsening domestic economic situation, the Harold Wilson government downscaled the British presence in Southeast Asia. For the second time, Singapore was left in the lurch, the first being the hasty retreat from the onslaught of the Japanese invading forces in 1941. These two events brought home to the leaders and people of Singapore that they had to take responsibility for their own survival and well-being. These searing experiences served as the genesis for several policies, including the decision to set up a citizen army, with National Service at its core. In the area of foreign affairs, Singapore decided to adopt a multi-directional approach. Singapore's first foreign minister, Mr S Rajaratnam, spelled out the policy of cultivating as many permanent friends as possible, given that it is not wise to formulate foreign policy on the basis of permanent enemies, in his first speech in Parliament as Foreign Minister.[11]

Already reeling from the effects of Separation, the Singapore government had to deal with the loss of the sizable financial contribution made by the British to the local economy. Thousands of workers and their families were dependent on employment in the bases.

Pleas by Mr Lee Kuan Yew and his colleagues to the British government to delay the withdrawal by a couple of years fell on deaf ears.

As part of the terms negotiated for the withdrawal from the bases, the British government gave Singapore a sum of £50 million, half of it as a grant, the other half as a soft loan. Taking it as a solace of some sort, the Singapore government used the money to address the socio-economic problems confronting the nation. The chief of these problems was unemployment. There was also the question of what to do with the bases. Information about the bases was lacking locally as the records were held in London. I recollect Permanent Secretary, Mr Pang Twee

---

[11] From email communication of 9 December 2018 with Irene Ng, author of *The Singapore Lion: A Biography of S Rajaratnam* (Institute of Southeast Asian Studies, 2010).

Pow, telling us that the information was wanted urgently. I was among a task force, headed by Deputy Secretary Wong Hung Khim, which worked overnight and produced the required information in a report, within a record time of 48 hours. Among other things, this information was to be the basis for the conversion of the British bases to civilian use. A Bases Economic Conversion Department (BECD) was headed by Mr Hon Sui Sen, with the title of Commissioner. Mr KR Chandra, P.S. Law, headed the Land and Facilities Department, while Mr JY Pillay was in charge of the economic side where he was tasked with, commercialising some of the facilities and workshops the British forces left behind. Among the accomplishments of BECD was the incorporation of Sembawang Shipyard to take over the dry-dock workshops and employees of the British Naval Base.

Like me, Mr JY Pillay had also moved from Kuala Lumpur in the early 1960s. The comparison ends there as Mr JY Pillay went on to scale the heights of the public and private sectors. His greatest achievement was the success story of Singapore Airlines. If ever a demonstration of the validity of Singapore's policy of "meritocracy" is needed, the life and achievements of Mr JY Pillay would serve that purpose admirably. Mr JY Pillay served as Chairman of the Council of Presidential Advisors for 18 years. He also stood in for the President when the President was away from the country. Simple in his tastes, his favourite restaurant is Madras New Woodlands at Upper Dickson Road, where he meets his friends regularly. He refers to the restaurant as "Woodies". Another one of his favourite meeting places is Annalakshmi, a vegetarian restaurant at Central Square. Occasionally, I am a beneficiary of his generosity. Mr JY Pillay recalls, "Actually, Woodies started as an aprestennis outing on weekend mornings. As age and infirmity caught up with us, the tennis was gradually dropped." (From his personal email communication with me dated 16 January 2019).

Another area that the Singapore government looked into, to address the fall-out from the consequences of the British withdrawal, was the promotion of tourism. Among other things, this required an urgent increase in trained manpower for the industry. Using a portion of the grant from the British government, a Hotel and Catering Training School was set up in Nassim Hill around 1968. As the project was also targeted at reducing unemployment, the Ministry of Labour was a key player and I was assigned to cover its interests in the project.

I am happy to see that the Hotel and Catering Training School has evolved into the prestigious SHATEC Institute of today. It was established in 1983. A recent publication, *Developing Hospitality Talent*, tells the story of how the Training School, initiated and developed by the late Mr Pakir Singh, is now compared to the Lausanne Hotel School (EHL) in Switzerland. As Madam Kay Kuok, president of the Singapore Hotel Association has put it,[12]

> ... in the last thirty years, SHATEC has forged ahead and carved for itself a brand name in hospitality, training and education, not only in Singapore but in the region as well.

---

[12] Raini Hamdi, *Developing Hospitality Talent* (Shatec, 2013) p 5 <https://epublishbyus.com/ebook/ebook?id=10033114#/6>

This is truly an illustration of how the mighty oak comes from the humble acorn.

On top of this, I was also tasked by the successive Permanent Secretaries to handle the Labour Ministry's external relations. This enabled me to travel to Geneva to participate in the annual International Labour Conference. However, my heart continued to yearn for the diplomatic career that my Permanent Secretaries, Mr Kwa Soon Chuan and Mr Lim Joo Hock, were reluctant to release me to. I suppose they found me handy in dealing with the foreign dignitaries coming to Singapore and dealing with matters relating to international relations.

However, when I heard that Mr Kwa himself was going to be transferred to the Ministry of Health, I went up to him and said, "You want me to stay but you are moving on!" Realising that I had set my mind on a diplomatic career, he allowed me to be transferred to the Ministry of Foreign Affairs.

CHAPTER 7

The Diplomatic Journey Begins

I joined the Ministry of Foreign Affairs on 1 August 1972 as a Grade VIII Officer. It was a very small outfit then, with Mr Rajaratnam as Minister, Mr GV Boggaars as the Permanent Secretary and Mr SR Nathan as the Deputy Secretary. Tan Boon Seng, Peter Chan, Barry Desker, Kemal Siddique and See Chak Mun were among the other officers in the Ministry. Mushahid Ali, Tan Seng Chye and Raymond Wong, Jayaletchimi, Mary Seet and Mark Hong were among the others who joined us later.

I was posted to the Southeast Asia Section, which dealt with regional countries. Seven months after joining the Ministry, I was sent on a diplomatic training course to Canberra, Australia. This was a specially designed course for Australian diplomats with provision for some foreign diplomats to be included in it. It was a great learning experience and also an introduction to the lively Australian way of life. Some of the course participants like John Buckley and Alexander Brooking became lifelong friends.

Besides the formal training, participants were also taken on tours within the country. In my case, I travelled with a group by air from

Canberra to Alice Springs. We then travelled by car to Ayers Rock, a 500-kilometre drive through the desert. Ayers Rock is regarded by native Australians as a sacred place.

The participants also went to Papua New Guinea and visited the highland area of Goroka, where the inhabitants lived in a primitive manner. Some of them went around naked, with only ash smeared on their bodies. We were invited to a meal in a village, where we witnessed the method of preparing the meal. A hole was dug in the ground, and subsequently, meat and vegetables were put in. The hole was then covered up and a fire was lit on top! Imagine that! After a few hours, the food was dug up and served. It was truly a once-in-a-lifetime experience.

Perhaps the most memorable tour, for a wine lover like me, was a drive from Canberra to Adelaide, where we stopped at every winery along the way and tasted the best of Australian wine. We made sure that we had a teetotaler in the group, who did the driving. At one particular winery, we were offered drops of a 100-year-old wine, which had become treacle by then. It was like drinking toffee, very mushy but nice!

At the end of the formal part of the course, the participants were sent to various Australian postings for on-the-job experience. I was initially posted to the Australian embassy in Ireland. However, as I had already been to Ireland on holiday, during the time I was in Kirkby, I asked for another posting. My request was granted, and I landed up in Ankara, Turkey. Little did I know then that I would be visiting Turkey two decades later, in an ambassadorial capacity.

My arrival in Ankara coincided with the Embassy's search to rent a holiday bungalow by the seaside. So, the First Secretary, one member of the local staff and I went to various parts of the Turkish coast to scout for a suitable location. The Turkish are very hospitable, always warm and welcoming to people from foreign lands. We stopped for the night in a small fishing village and had some light snacks to sustain ourselves in the afternoon. We told the restaurant owner that we would be back for dinner. Upon our return, we were pleasantly surprised to find that he had gone out to sea and caught some fish for our dinner! These are the small things that stick in one's mind.

All in all, the diplomatic training experience provided by the Australian government was a very pleasant one, with points learned and friendships forged.

Upon my return to the Ministry, I was told that I would be posted to Kuala Lumpur as the Deputy High Commissioner. I felt rather uneasy about this, as it was less than five years since I had come from Malaysia. I was not sure how the Malaysians would react to my return, and I was concerned that this would have an adverse effect on my performance. I expressed my concerns to Mr Bogaars. Understanding my concerns, he agreed that it was not a wise move to post me to Kuala Lumpur at that point in time.

Fate, however, ensured that I would return to Malaysia three decades later as the High Commissioner!

CHAPTER 8

My Southern Odyssey

Thanks to Mr Boggaar's intervention, I was posted to the Singapore Embassy in Jakarta as the Counsellor, also known as the Deputy Head of Mission, in 1973. The Head of Mission was Ambassador Lee Khoon Choy. He was a former Senior Minister of State in the Singapore government. A multi-talented person, he was a pianist, calligrapher, golfer and an author. His book, *Indonesia: Between Myth and Reality*,[13] was a masterpiece and became essential reading for an understanding of Indonesian culture and politics. Ambassador Lee's affable ways and keen interest in *Kerpercayaan*, a form of spiritual belief practised mainly in Java, made him well-liked amongst Indonesians from all ranks of life. Two of his closest contacts were General Sujono Humardani and General Ali Murtopo. They were patrons of the Centre for Strategic and International Studies (CSIS), the leading think tank in Indonesia.

My predecessor in the post of Counsellor was Kemal Siddique, popularly known as Tony. He and his charming wife, Sharon, were to become lifelong friends.

[13] Lee Khoon Choy, *Indonesia: Between Myth and Reality* (Nile & Mackenzie, 1976).

Bilateral relations between Indonesia and Singapore were correct, though tense at times. This was largely on account of an incident in 1968, when two Indonesian Marines had been hanged for planting a bomb inside MacDonald House in 1965. It had resulted in the deaths of three persons and injured at least 33 others. This incident was to be known later as the MacDonald House bombing. The two Indonesians were charged with murder, put on to trial and executed by hanging. This enraged the Indonesians. Hence, it was a very turbulent time, but ambassadors Mr PS Raman and Mr Lee Khoon Choy were able to manage the situation.

In 1973, the then Prime Minister Lee Kuan Yew visited Jakarta in an effort to thaw the diplomatic chill that had settled over the two countries. Ambassador Lee suggested that some flowers be sprinkled on the graves of the two Marine Commandos in the Heroes Cemetery in Kalibata. The Indonesians interpreted this gesture as a form of apology by Singapore. For Singapore, it was to indicate "let bygones be bygones". This single act helped improve relations, both between the countries and the leaders, Mr Lee Kuan Yew and President Suharto. Hence, by the time I arrived, much of the turbulence in bilateral relations had subsided.

Long after both leaders had left the political stage, they continued to maintain their friendship. Mr Lee Kuan Yew visited President Suharto even after both of them had left active politics. In his memoirs, *From Third World to First*, Mr Lee has written about Suharto's legacy vis-à-vis ASEAN, as follows:[14]

[14] Lee Kuan Yew, *From Third World to First – The Singapore Story: 1965–2000* (Marshall Cavendish Editions, 2014) pp 369–370.

> The role of President Suharto was crucial for the success of Asean. After some false starts by pushy Indonesian officials, Suharto moderated the approach to one diametrically different from India's vis-à-vis the member countries of SAARC (South Asia Association for Regional Cooperation). Under Suharto, Indonesia did not act like a hegemon. It did not insist on its point of view but took into consideration the policies and interests of other members. This made it possible for the others to accept Indonesia as first among equals.

Due to my grounding in the Malay language, I was able to pick up Bahasa Indonesia quickly. This enabled me to establish contacts with all levels of Indonesian society. Also, because of Ambassador Lee's standing in the diplomatic world, the Singapore mission was highly regarded, both by the Indonesians and the diplomatic community. We were constantly approached by other missions and visitors for readings on the domestic political situation in Indonesia as well as on issues in international relations in the region.

My main source of information was from friends in CSIS (Centre for Strategic and International Studies). Among my contacts in the CSIS were Mr Harry Chan Silalahi, Mr Yusuf Wanandi and Ms Clara Joewono. As they were close to the seat of power, they were vital sources of information. We also became good friends in the process.

The most notable event during my three-year stay in Indonesia was its annexation of East Timor, which took place much against the climate of international opinion, including Singapore's. Indonesia's fear was that East Timor would become a thorn in its side, just as in the case of Cuba, for the USA.

A few days before the invasion, a journalist friend of mine alerted me that the invasion was going to take place. He advised that I convey the news to Singapore, with a hint that Singapore should support Indonesia's actions. However, no less a person than Foreign Minister Mr Rajaratnam stated that it would be a folly for Indonesia to annex East Timor. This issue was to cause a temporary blip in our bilateral relations, which was resolved by the passage of time.

The posting to Indonesia also enabled my family and me to travel quite extensively in this vast country. On one occasion, my friend Mr Alvin Kwan and I drove all the way from Jakarta to Bali! In those days, it was very easy to travel around. You could go into any village, stay and eat the local food.

We were struck by the rich Indic culture that was to be seen everywhere. Statues from the Hindu epics of the *Ramayana* and *Mahabharata* were also to be seen in major roundabouts and prominent buildings like the Merdeka Palace in Jakarta. Names and places originated in the Sanskrit language, and, of course, Bali was the quintessence of Indonesian Hinduism. No wonder Poet Laureate, Rabindranath Tagore, had said, during his trip to Java in 1927 that he saw Hinduism everywhere but did not recognise it.

All in all, my posting to Indonesia was an enriching experience and helped me to understand the dynamics of Singapore's relations with its southern neighbour.

I learned an important lesson during this posting about human interaction: no matter how busy you are, you always make time for people. One day, I rang up Mr Ali Alatas, who was then Secretary to the Foreign Minister, Adam Malek, for an appointment for the next day and he said "Why tomorrow? Come now if you can."

In another incident, I was trying to get an appointment with an Indonesian officer and was constantly told by his secretary that "Bapak sibok". (He is busy.) I decided to try another tactic. I invited him for an afternoon game of golf. I got an appointment right away! I had only wanted 45 minutes but I ended up spending four hours with him playing golf. Needless to say, my golf game showed improvement during my time in Jakarta. Likewise, golf was also of help to me in other stages of my career.

Barry Desker succeeded me as Counsellor. He was to return as Ambassador with his wife, Peggy, and served in Indonesia for several years. Later, he went on to head the Rajaratnam School of International Studies (RSIS) at Nanyang Technological University. Mr Edward Lee, another colleague in the mission, returned and served as Ambassador for over 13 years. David Low and his wife, Peck Chin, were also close friends. Another dear friend of mine was the late KK Menon, the father of current Chief Justice Sundaresh Menon. He was Personal Assistant to Ambassador Lee.

Padmini and I also interacted with a wide circle of friends in Indonesia, including Ananda Sivaraman and his artist wife, Shanti, and their children Geetha and Madhu. We continue to remain close friends and we visit one another in Kerala and Singapore. Very generous and endearing, they have a special place in our hearts.

I returned to Singapore in 1976 and was posted to the West European Directorate as Deputy Director. The Directorate was headed by Kemal Siddique and was charged with monitoring of the West European countries. D Murugan was the Country Desk Officer. The three of us, Kemal Siddique, D Murugan and I formed an effective team and were complimented by the late Mr Nathan on our presentation at the Ministry's "morning prayers". Every morning, Mr Nathan would chair a meeting of senior officers where each Desk would have to present its review of the situation in the countries under their charge. Heaven help officers who were unprepared or woolly in their presentations. They were pulled up by remarks such as "cut out the palavar and come to the point". These "morning prayers", as they came to be fondly known, became an institution which, I believe, is still continued today.

CHAPTER 9

To the Land of Tolstoy and Dostoevsky

After two years in Headquarters, I was posted to Moscow, the land of Tolstoy and Dostoevsky, two of my favourite authors. It was a dream come true to be posted to the land that produced such literary geniuses.

Prior to my posting, I was sent by the Ministry of Foreign Affairs for a three-month summer study course in Language and Soviet Studies at Georgetown University in Washington DC. This equipped me with a basic understanding of the Russian language and background on Soviet and East European affairs. It proved to be useful in my interactions with both Soviet officials and the diplomatic community. The Heads of the Moscow Mission were Mr Joseph Conceiceo and Mr Eddie Ho, the father of Peter Ho, who was to become a highly respected Permanent Secretary. Peter Ho went on to become Singapore's Head of Civil Service.

My posting to Moscow coincided with the height of the Cold War period, and the task of the Mission was essentially to monitor superpower politics, especially the Soviet Union's relations with

China and the inroads that Soviet-led communism was making into Southeast Asia. It was also a time of great internal leadership changes in Moscow. I was to witness the state funerals of Leonid Brezhnev, Konstantin Chernenko and Yury Andropov. They were staged as massive events with millions of mourners all over the USSR participating in the ceremonies. State funerals provided occasions for students of Sovietology to study current and future power structures. The moment a leader died, the first thing the government did was to announce the composition of the Funeral Committee. It would normally be headed by the deceased's successor, and the allocation of responsibilities for the funeral ceremony was closely watched for clues on the future positions of Politburo members within the Party. Foreign diplomats went to great lengths to study these developments, in an effort to predict how power would shift with the advent of a new leader.

As a person of Indian origin, I was frequently mistaken to be an Indian diplomat. This proved to be a blessing in disguise, given the very cordial relations between the Soviet Union and India. Ashwini Devare, in her recently published book, *Lost at 15, Found at 50,* has described the relationship as follows:[15]

> Indo-Soviet relations were on an upswing, a honeymoon period, and a good time for Indians to be in Moscow. Indians enjoyed a special relationship with the Soviets, a friendship that coincided

---

[15] Ashwini Devare, *Lost at 15, Found at 50* (Marshall Cavendish Editions, 2019) p 29

> with the start of the Cold War, when both superpowers began aggressively wooing former colonies to recruit them into their 'camp'.

The following is a story to illustrate just how good that relationship was at that time.

In October 1980, I had gone to Tashkent, Uzbekistan, back when it was still part of the Soviet Union. It was a guided tour for foreign diplomats. While I was there, I was kept under close watch as all foreign diplomats were, and I even had a minder attached to me. However, I managed to give him the slip and entered a café in the town. I ordered a beer and, before I knew it, a few locals came around saying, "Oi, Indianski, Indianski!" meaning that I was an Indian and we were brothers. Before long, we were drinking, toasting and singing together. My newfound friends could sing Hindi songs from Raj Kapoor's movies very well, and soon we were making so much noise that a policeman came around. He asked about the commotion and they explained that we were celebrating the friendship between two great nations. The policeman just said, "Okay, okay, don't make too much noise," and left. That was a memorable occasion indeed.

A notable point during my time in the USSR was the Soviet invasion of Afghanistan. I was at a Christmas party hosted by a diplomatic colleague on the evening of 26 December 1979. Suddenly, some of us noticed that the diplomats from the Western missions were leaving, one by one. At that time, we did not know what was happening. The next day, we learned that the Soviet Union had invaded Afghanistan.

Over the next four years, diplomats in Moscow were kept busy with monitoring the albatross that the Soviet government had brought unto itself!

Another casualty for the Soviets was the international boycott of the 1980 Olympics held in Moscow. As Singapore was among the boycotting countries, Mission staff had to be content with hearing the roars coming from the stadium, which was a few miles away from the residences.

The general impression under communism was that everything was equal and everything was fair. The reality of it was that the Soviet Union was one of the most class-ridden and unequal of societies. Those who belonged to the Nomenklatura – a group of people who were the insiders – lived well and had special shops to shop in, and special cars to drive, among other privileges.

By the same token, foreigners also lived relatively well because they had access to foreign exchange shops, with goods imported from Sweden and Denmark. Foreigners could go to the Bolshoi Ballet or to the circus as many times as they liked, while ordinary Russian folks found it difficult to visit either of these places even once in their lifetime.

I was to experience firsthand examples of espionage that a reader of John le Carre's novels would find familiar. For example, a whole panel of "bugs" was found in the Ambassador's office. There was also an incident about the American ambassador's heels being planted with listening devices. Talk was that the maids would take out the heels, put the microphones in and then reassemble the shoes.

I also experienced the trauma of one of our embassy staff being compromised by Soviet intelligence agents. He was sent back, dismissed from service and sentenced to several years in prison.

As we were concerned about the children's education, my wife and the boys did not join me in my Moscow posting. Murali was ten years old and Sashi was barely six. We did not want to interrupt their education. My wife and I also thought that the two years would fly by quickly with me flying in to visit them once a year and they would come over during the school holidays. Thankfully, we had good friends in the Embassy such as Nithi and Maud, as well as Emily and her husband, Joseph. We became a close knit "family".

My knowledge of the Russian language came in handy in making friends as well. I was often invited by the warmhearted Malaysian ambassador, KT Ratnam, and his deputy, Emam Mohd Hanif, to dinner at fancy restaurants in Moscow. They depended on me to order our meals. That was until they discovered one day that the English translations to the menu were written in small print below each item. Nevertheless, the invitations did not stop!

Both Ambassador KT Ratnam and Emam Mohd Hanif were later posted to Singapore.

One of the compensations of serving in Moscow was being able to travel to any one of the nearby capitals of the western countries. This was on account of the fact that the Soviet Union was considered a hard posting. The favourite choice was London, of course.

We came back with goodies such as nylon stockings, chocolates, coffee powder, which we used to get on the right side of the female staff in Gastranom, the shop with high-quality foreign goods. In return, the staff would alert us to any forthcoming shipment from Copenhagen or Stockholm. If you missed one shipment, it would be a two or three-month wait for the next shipment.

One funny incident that I recall was when I had made an appointment to meet a US diplomat in his embassy. As I was about to leave to keep my appointment, I received an alert from my contact in Gastranom that a fresh supply of coffee powder and other essentials had arrived. I told Emily to reschedule the appointment. The US diplomat readily agreed to my request. Half an hour later, both the US diplomat and I found ourselves at the Gastranom looking at the goods on display from the latest shipment!

Within Moscow, travel for foreigners was restricted. As Ashwini Devare describes in her book,[16] "you couldn't go beyond forty

[16] Ashwini Devare, *Lost at 15, Found at 50* (Marshall Cavendish Editions, 2019) p 28.

kilometres without permission" and "many areas were completely off-limits". One day, my colleague in the mission, Alan Khoo, and I decided to test whether this was really true. Travelling 50 kilometres out of Moscow, we turned into a side road to have a coffee break. Within ten minutes, a security patrol guard found us and asked what we were doing. Giving a severe warning, they allowed us to return to Moscow. Such was life in the then Soviet paradise.

CHAPTER 10

To be in England

On my return to Singapore, I served in the Political Division of the West European Directorate of the Ministry. A year later, I was posted as the Deputy High Commissioner of our mission in London. This was a particularly enjoyable posting as living and working was easy and comfortable. It brought back memories of my earlier sojourn in the UK as a trainee teacher. This time, I had a wife and two children with me. However, my memory of England had not changed and brought to mind the poem of Robert Browning:

> Oh, to be in England
> Now that April's there,
> And whoever wakes in England
> Sees, some morning, unaware,
> That the lowest boughs and the
> brushwood sheaf
> Round the elm-tree bole are in tiny leaf,
> While the chaffinch sings on the orchard bough
> In England – now!

It was also an educationally productive posting for my family as I was able to earn a Masters degree from the School of Oriental and African Studies (SOAS).

With the loss of the empire, the UK was no longer in the front ranks of great powers. However, the universities and research institutes were reservoirs of intellectual capital. By tapping on the scholars in these institutes, I was able to send back useful reports on regional and international affairs. It was here that I met scholars of international repute, like the late Professor Michael Leifer and Professor Michael Yehuda of the London School of Economics (LSE), as well as Professor Ralph Hunt and Professor Robert Taylor of SOAS.

Of my two sons, my elder one, Murali, went to a public school, while Sashi attended a state school. They continued their education in the UK, with Murali reading law at Warwick University and the Middle Temple, while Sashi did his BSc degree at Imperial College and PhD in molecular neuroscience at King's College London. On 7 January 2019, Murali, along with three of his colleagues, Dato Jude Benny, John Sze and Danny Chua from the law firm Joseph Tan Jude Benny, obtained accreditation as Senior Accredited Specialists in Maritime and Shipping Law by the Singapore Academy of Law. Sashi is now the Director and Head of Biology at the Nanyang Technological University. I am happy that both my sons have used, in the words of DPM Tharman Shanmugaratnam, "the educational elevator" to be where they are today.

My wife also took the opportunity to take a course in the field of Special Education and earned a Certificate of Teaching from the University of London. This was to serve her well when she returned to Singapore and obtained a teaching job at Dover Court International School. That is how all four members of the family were engaged in learning at the same time while we were in London.

The period in London was sweetened by the entry of our third "son", Benji. On account of the pestering from my two boys, the whole family went to a kennel in North London where there were ten puppies in a basket. One of them looked up at Murali and it was love at first sight. Benji became part of the family for the next 15 years. Highly intelligent and sensitive, he enriched our lives beyond measure. Visitors who came to the house, like David Chin from then Trade Development Board (Singapore), never forgot him. Even now, David says that he has never seen anyone play football like Benji!

There is a funny story about Benji. When we moved back to Singapore, we lived in an apartment in Marine Vista in the East Coast. Having lived in a bungalow with a garden in London, Benji did not adapt well to living in an apartment. Every morning, the maid would bring him down for his walk and every day it was a struggle to get him back into the flat. One day, he just disappeared.

The maid had brought him down and he slipped away. We went searching high and low for him. Finally, Sashi spotted him outside

McDonalds at East Coast Parkway. He was surrounded by newfound companions. We could not understand how, with his leash intact, he could have crossed the East Coast Parkway (ECP). When he saw Sashi, he turned his face away, thus making his displeasure known over the living arrangements.

Traumatised by this incident, my wife put her foot down and said, "We move to a landed property." First, we rented a place in Moonbeam Walk in Holland Road. Later on, we bought a place in the same neighbourhood.

As we were searching for a house to buy, an estate agent said that there was a house for viewing close to us. We asked her how many bathrooms there were in the house. When we heard the answer, we rejected the house. The agent persuaded us to take a look. The moment we stepped into the house, we fell in love with it and the red brick English-style dining room. It was also a corner property that gave us more privacy and a reasonably-sized garden. Over time, the property has appreciated in value. As it was due to Benji that we made this investment, we named him our "million-dollar dog".

When I was later posted to Kuala Lumpur, my wife felt that Benji would find it difficult to be quarantined for a lengthy period of time. We managed to work out a deal with the quarantine authorities in Subang Airport in Kuala Lumpur to the effect that he would be quarantined for one week in the airport holding area, and for the rest of the time he would be restricted to the garden in the High Commissioner's Residence in Kuala Lumpur. As it was the first time that Benji was separated from the family, Murali and Sashi, who were by then working in Singapore, took leave to be with him in KL. So what transpired was that Benji moved first into the Residence, and I followed!

Benji accompanied us to all our subsequent postings and he finally ended his days in Kuala Lumpur. He had given us 15 years of unconditional love and affection. My wife refuses to entertain the thought of having another dog.

With Raju Suppiah, college mate in Kirkby College at the Rain Tree Race Course, Liverpool, United Kingdom (circa 1956)

Kesavapany (*standing, second from left*) with family members (August 1958)

Pany (*back row, centre*) and Padmini (*front row, extreme right*) with Hindu Youth Organisation committee members in Penang, Malaysia, during a visit to the School for the Blind (1961)

Pany and Padmini (1962)

Pany and Padmini's wedding (26 January 1963)

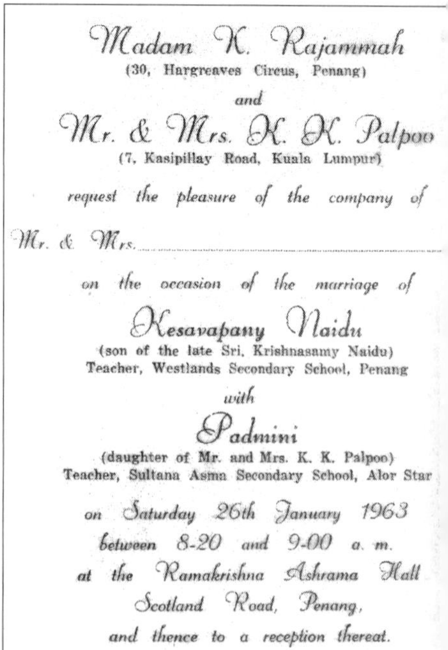

Madam K. Rajammah
(30, Hargreaves Circus, Penang)
and
Mr. & Mrs. K. K. Palpoo
(7, Kasipillay Road, Kuala Lumpur)
request the pleasure of the company of
Mr. & Mrs. ....
on the occasion of the marriage of
Kesavapany Naidu
(son of the late Sri. Krishnasamy Naidu)
Teacher, Westlands Secondary School, Penang
with
Padmini
(daughter of Mr. and Mrs. K. K. Palpoo)
Teacher, Sultana Asma Secondary School, Alor Star
on Saturday 26th January 1963
between 8-20 and 9-00 a. m.
at the Ramakrishna Ashrama Hall
Scotland Road, Penang,
and thence to a reception thereat.

Pany and Padmini's wedding invitation (1963)

Wedding at Penang, Malaysia (26 January 1963)

With the family on my graduation from the University of Malaya, *back row, from left*: Padmini Kesavapany, Shanti, Kesavapany; *front row, from left*: Radhakrishnapany, Kothandapany, Jayanthi, Thasarathapany, Chandra Mohan Pany (1966)

Ambassador Kesavapany receiving his degree from Tunku Abdul Rahman (1967)

With Mr Kwa Soon Chuan, Permanent Secretary, Ministry of Labour, at the International Labour Organisation (ILO) General Assembly in Geneva (circa 1970)

Ambassador Kesavapany with fellow course mates at Ayers Rock, Australia (1972)

From left: President Suharto, interpreter, the late Lee Khoon Choy and Ambassador Kesavapany (1976)

Pany and Padmini with Murali Pany and the late Mr B Rajaram

Ambassador Kesavapany and Sashi Pany (1978)

Sashi and Murali Pany at Changi Airport

Benji (1983)

Ambassador Kesavapany being awarded the Pingat Bakti Masyarakat (PBM) from President SR Nathan (2001)

Pany and Padmini on their way to Buckingham Palace (1982)

Padmini Kesavapany at Dover Court Preparatory School on United Nations Day (1990)

Singapore's participation at the International Garden Festival in Liverpool, United Kingdom (circa 1984)

From left: Leow Siu Lin, the late Chia Cheong Fook, Chandra Das and Ambassador Kesavapany in Wellington, New Zealand (1988)

Sashi Pany on the occasion of his passing out parade from the Officer Cadet School (circa 1991)

Kesavapany presenting credentials to Mr Jan Martenson, the Director-General of the United Nations Office in Geneva (17 January 1992)

Presenting credentials to His Excellency the President of Turkey, Turgut Ozal (1992)

With the Singapore delegation to the UN Conference on Environment and Development led by Ambassador Tommy Koh (June 1992)

Murali Pany graduating from the University of Warwick, England (June 1994)

Murali Pany's graduation at the University of Warwick (June 1994)

President Tony Tan and group at Davos, Switzerland (1994/1995)

Ambassador Kesavapany and his beloved Benji in Geneva (1995)

Transformation of GATT to WTO (*from left*): Ambassador Zahran, Ambassador Kesavapany, Renato Ruggerio, Peter Sutherland (1995)

Honoured by Dr R Theyvendran, President of the Sri Senpaga Vinayagar Temple

Greeting the Yang di-Pertuan Agong of Malaysia and Raja Permaisuri Agong of Malaysia on the occasion of the presentation of credentials (1997)

On the occasion of the presentation of credentials by Ambassador Kesavapany to the Yang di-Pertuan Agong of Malaysia (1997)

Presentation of credentials by High Commissioner Kesavapany to the Yang di-Pertuan Agong of Malaysia (1997)

Ambassador Kesavapany – the golfer in action (2000)

Ambassador Kesavapany (circa 2000)

Honoured by the Hashemite Kingdom of Jordan with the title First Class Order of Independence (14 March 2000)

Pany and Padmini invested with the Order of the Hashemite Kingdom of Jordan (circa 2000)

Padmini Kesavapany accompanying the late Mrs Lee Kuan Yew to a tea reception in Kuala Lumpur hosted by Tun Dr Siti Hasmah binti Haji Mohamad Ali (2000)

Padmini Kesavapany with Tun Dr Siti Hasmah binti Haji Mohamad Ali at a tea reception in Kuala Lumpur (2000)

Pany and Padmini with Minister for Foreign Affairs, Mr K Shanmugam at the Ministry of Foreign Affairs

بسم الله الرحمن الرحيم

عبد الله

نحن بنعمة الله عبد الله الثاني ابن الحسين ملك المملكة الأردنية الهاشمية

تقديراً للصفات الحميدة التي يتحلى بها سعادة السيد ك. كيسافاباني سفير جمهورية سنغافورة السابق
لدى الأمم المتحدة / جنيف، والجهود المتواصلة والخدمات المتميزة التي أبداها خلال المفاوضات الأردنية
مع لجنة العمل في منظمة التجارة العالمية، والتي أسفرت عن انضمام الأردن إلى هذه المنظمة، فقد
قلدناه وسام الاستقلال من الدرجة الأولى، وأمرنا بإصدار هذه البراءة من ديواننا الملكي
الهاشمي إيذاناً بذلك.

صدر عن قصر بسمان الزاهر في عمان في اليوم الثامن من شهر ذي الحجة سنة ألف وأربعمائة وعشرين هجرية
الموافق لليوم الرابع عشر من شهر آذار سنة ألفين ميلادية.

بأمر جلالة مولاي الملك المعظم

رئيس الديوان الملكي الهاشمي

In the name of God

We, Abdullah the Second son of Al-Hussein, King of the Hashemite Kingdom of Jordan, adorned H E Mr K Kesavapany, former Singapore Ambassador to the United Nations in Geneva, the First Class Order of Independence, in appreciation of his good characteristics, continuous efforts and distinguished services that he showed during the Jordanian negotiations with the World Trade Organisation (WTO), Accessions Committee, which resulted in Jordan joining the WTO. This Merit was issued from our Hashemite Royal Cabinet.

Issued from our Besman Palace in Amman on 14 March 2000

At the order of HRH

(Abdullah)

Signed

Chief of the Hashemite Royal Cabinet

Pany and Padmini with the late Minister Mentor Lee Kuan Yew and the late Mrs Lee Kuan Yew at Rumah Temasek, Kuala Lumpur (17 August 2000)

With Professor Wang Gungwu, Professor Tommy Koh and Professor Kishore Mahbubani

Pany and Padmini with Ambassador Dasho Paljor Dorji (also known as Benji) in Paro, the Tiger's Nest, Bhutan (circa 2000)

Ambassador Dasho Paljor Dorji with Ambassador Kesavapany at the Tiger's Nest (circa 2000)

Ambassador Kesavapany with Tiger Woods (*right*) at the Mines Resort, Kuala Lumpur (circa 2000)

During a call on the King of Jordan, His Majesty King Abdullah II of Jordan in Amman, Jordan (circa late 2000s)

During a call on the King of Jordan, His Majesty King Abdullah II of Jordan in Amman, Jordan (circa late 2000s)

With Premjit Sadasivan and Rosman Ithnin in Bedouin camp in Petra, Jordan (circa 2000)

Pany and Padmini in traditional Kerala attire at a wedding in Thiruvananthapuram (Trivandrum), Kerala (circa 2000)

Sashi Pany graduating from King's College London with a PhD in Molecular Neuroscience (2001)

Wedding reception of Dr Sashi Pany & Geetha Naidu at the Royal Selangor Club, Kuala Lumpur (June 2002)

The late SR Nathan with Ambassador Kesavapany (2002)

With the late Mr SR Nathan and Mrs Umi Nathan (2002)

Ambassador Kesavapany with Wong Kan Seng, Abdullah Badawi, Professor S Jayakumar, amongst others, at Abdullah Badawi's home in KL after his daughter's wedding

Ambassador Kesavapany with Wong Kang Seng and other delegates in Geneva

Welcoming Princess of Thailand, Sirindhorn, at ISEAS (2004)

Greeting Dr Mahathir Bin Mohamad, Prime Minister of Malaysia, at the Hari Raya Open House in Kuala Lumpur (2004)

Murali and Jyoti on holiday in Amsterdam (circa 2005)

Ambassador Kesavapany with faculty members of the Lee Kuan Yew School of Public Policy (2005)

With the sixth President of Singapore, Mr SR Nathan and Mrs Umi Nathan during a reception at the Istana (24 November 2005)

Ambassador Kesavapany's 70th birthday celebrations with family and friends (2006)

One of Ambassador Kesavapany's favourite photos of his travels: the ruins of Angkor Wat

Pany and Padmini with Professor S Jayakumar and Mrs Jayakumar

Pany and Padmini with the fourth President of Singapore, Mr Wee Kim Wee and Mrs Wee Kim Wee

Her Majesty Queen Elizabeth II and Prince Philip with the High Commissioners of the Commonwealth in Kuala Lumpur

The late Mr SR Nathan meeting members of the Inter-Religious Organisation (IRO) Council at the Istana (20 December 2009)

Book launch of Sugata Bose's *His Majesty's Opponent: Subhas Chandra Bose and India's Struggle against Empire* (2011)

Launch of a book by the late Mr SR Nathan (20 May 2011)

Portrait of Mr Kesavapany at ISEAS (2012)

Ambassador Kesavapany with his family on his 78th birthday (2014)

Leading a Singapore International Foundation (SIF) delegation to meet with Mochamad Ridwan Kamil, the Mayor of Bandung (2015)

Pany and Padmini at their residence at Holland Village (2016)

Kirkbyites at the unveiling of the commemorative plaque at the Malayan Teachers Training College (MTTC) Kirkby site (31 August 2017)

Grandpa celebrating his 81st birthday with the apples of his eyes: Jaynna Sashi Pany and Kishan Sashi Pany (2017)

Official launch of the Abdul Kalam Vision Society, K Kesavapany with His Excellency Jawed Ashraf, High Commissioner of India to Singapore and Dr Ponraj (21 July 2018)

Mr and Mrs Kesavapany at the Abdul Kalam Vision Society's "Keeping Little India Clean and Beautiful" event (14 October 2018)

From left: Sashi Pany, Jaynna, Kesavapany, Kishan and Geetha Naidu (2018)

Bringing cheer to the residents at Sree Narayana Mission on Deepavali – the event was jointly organised by the Abdul Kalam Vision Society and the Singapore Indian Association with the support of Mr Nirmalan Pillay. Guest of honour for the event: Mr Ali Mohamed Irshad, Nominated MP (4 November 2018)

Grandchildren (from left): Kishan Sashi Pany and Jaynna Sashi Pany (2018)

Inter-Religious Organisation (IRO) members meeting Her Excellency President Halimah Yacob shortly after her inauguration as President of Singapore (2018)

Kirkby Reunion 2018 (Puteri Pan Pacific Johor Bahru)

In remembrance of the immersion of Gandhi's ashes at Clifford Pier (*from left to right*: HE Jawed Hasraf, Kesavapany, Swami Vimokshananda, ESM Goh Chok Tong, PM Narendra Modi, Ameer Ali, Rustom Ghadiali and Reverend Ven Seck Kwang Peng) (2018)

Prince Charles' visit to the Inter-Religious Organization (2018)

CHAPTER 11

Tending to the Region

On 4 April 1988, I was posted as Director of the ASEAN Directorate. This job required a lot of travelling in view of the many meetings that took place in various ASEAN capitals and elsewhere around the globe. Understandably, it took a toll on family life, particularly when the children were growing up.

One of the compensations was the opportunities to indulge in my passion, playing golf. I was fortunate to have several golfers among my fellow Directors-General (DGs) from the other ASEAN countries, including Ajit Singh of Malaysia, Agus Termazi of Indonesia and Hamid of Brunei. Much of the decision-making was done on the golf course which was later endorsed at formal meetings. Any of the DGs not in the golfing group found himself in the dark as to how the decisions had been arrived at.

When Toh Hock Ghim joined me as the Deputy Director, the first thing I told him was to "go and buy a set of golf clubs and learn the game. Reading the files can wait." Hock Ghim took over from me as Director. He went on to Hong Kong to serve as Commissioner General. Now in the corporate sector, he serves on the boards of several companies.

His wife, Amy, was there for him at a defining moment of his life, but that is his story to tell.

The ASEAN Directorate yielded a rich harvest of friends, including Ong Lu King, Puvirasa, Sivaprasathan, Thiru, Yunus, KP Menon, among others. Florence Chang, my first ever Personal Assistant, was kind and solicitous.

During my time in the ASEAN Directorate, I was able to play a part in restoring ASEAN-India ties. As a result of the differing positions on the issue of the Vietnamese occupation of Cambodia, ties between ASEAN and India became estranged. However, with Vietnam's withdrawal of its troops from Cambodia, this obstacle ended. During a golf game at the Singapore Island Country Club (Bukit Course), I suggested to then Indian High Commissioner, Yogesh Tiwari, that India send a note on wanting to restore ties with ASEAN. High Commissioner Tiwari followed up on my suggestion and since then, ASEAN-India relations have grown from strength to strength.

The ASEAN directorate was also responsible for the ministry's Technical Assistance Programme run by MFA. I was involved in the inauguration of the Third Country Training Program (TCTP) in association with the Japan International Cooperation Agency (JICA). The Japanese were training people from developing countries in Japan. However, the costs of travelling and accommodation were high. Hence, we suggested to the Japanese officials that a midway point, where travel and accommodation would be cheaper and where cultures would be more similar and easier for trainees to adapt, would be a better choice. This way, more people could be trained with savings on resources. The aim of the programme was to provide joint technical assistance to developing countries, by training government officials from across the world in diverse fields such as public governance, trade promotion, urban planning, education and healthcare.

During my term, the TCTP ran over a hundred courses. It was to evolve into the Singapore Co-operation Programme, which extends technical assistance to over 130 countries today. This is a concrete example of Singapore sharing its developmental experiences with the international community.

After three years in the ASEAN Directorate, I moved on to the International Relations Directorate in 1990. It was just to be for a year. It was here that I came into close contact with Ambassador Tommy Koh, with whom I went to several conferences, including the Earth Summit in Rio de Janerio. Ambassador Tommy Koh was the chairman of this conference, which resulted in a landmark agreement on climate change and the environment. It was an education in life to work in close proximity with Tommy, as he was affectionately called by all. When you went on a delegation with him, his first concern was how the delegates in his team were going to be looked after. He was particular about meals and would personally choose the restaurants and menus of where the delegates would dine.

Tommy had the magical touch of being able to connect with the highest in the land and *hoi polloi*. At the United Nations, he would greet and shake hands with everyone he came into contact with, including the security guards.

There were many calls for him to stand for the post of the United Nations' Secretary General. He was everyone's choice. However, in deference to his friend, the incumbent Boutros Boutros-Ghali, who was seeking re-election in 1997, Tommy declined to put himself up for the post. Singapore lost its chance to have a Singaporean as the Head of the most important international organisation and the United Nations missed the opportunity of having onboard one of the most highly skilled diplomats in the world.

Our paths have since crossed and criss-crossed over many years and on many occasions. Tommy taught me how to wear the mantle of greatness and be humble at all times. Tommy is a man for all seasons. For instance, upon my request, he launched the book, *From Kerala to Singapore: Voices from the Singapore Malayalee Community*[17] by Anitha Devi Pillai and Puva Arumugam in 2017. He addressed the crowd with the opening line, "My dear Indian brothers and sisters", and immediately connected with the audience. In his speech, he acknowledged all who were there and those who were not there.

His wife, Siew Aing, is equally gracious. On one occasion, I went to the Pinetree Club on Stevens Road to have lunch with Tommy. Foolishly,

[17] Anitha Devi Pillai & Puva Arumugam, *From Kerala to Singapore: Voices from the Singapore Malayalee Community* (Marshall Cavendish Editions, 2017).

I got the date wrong. Siew Aing happened to be there and she invited me to have lunch with her. We had a good conversation.

Tommy has touched many lives and shaped many institutions, particularly in the cultural sphere like the National Arts Council and the National Gallery. He has stood by his principles on the issue of the repeal of section 377A of the Penal Code. Lately, he has taken on the task of highlighting the issue of a minimum wage.

CHAPTER 12

Diplomacy in Geneva

One fine afternoon, while I was dozing in my office following a heavy lunch at Samy's Curry at Dempsey, the telephone rang. Patsy, the PA to the Permanent Secretary (PS), Mr Peter Chan, said, "PS wants to see you."

Not a person known for small talk, Peter informed me of the decision to post me to Geneva. I was taken aback as I had no knowledge of economics or commerce, particularly trade-related matters. Obviously, Peter knew something about me that I did not. As a Foreign Service Officer goes wherever he is asked to go, on 28 December 1991, my wife and I, with Benji in tow, landed in Geneva.

Geneva is the home of key international institutions like the UN agencies and the General Agreement on Tariffs and Trades (GATT). The Residence was a pleasant house, with a garden and a pool. Benji was happiest of us all as he could run around to his heart's content. Also, the golf course in Colugny was only ten minutes away from the Residence, which made me rather happy.

Taking over from Ambassador See Chak Mun, I had to quickly learn both the content of the issues involved and negotiation techniques. I also had to familiarise myself with the movers and shakers in the organisation. On account of the Singapore Permanent Mission's high reputation, built up by my predecessors Chew Tai Soo and See Chak Mun, I found myself being welcomed into the key negotiating groups.

Workwise, the atmosphere in GATT was gloomy. The Uruguay Round Negotiations, which had commenced with much pomp and ceremony in Punta del Este in September 1986, were stalled. Despite the best efforts of Director-General Arthur Dunkel and the resident GATT ambassadors, no headway could be made. Several ministerial meetings convened to break the deadlock met with no success.

Dunkel, a Swiss civil servant, had a reputation for solid work but he could not get the process moving as the negotiations were largely in the hands of the so-called Quad, which comprised of the USA, Canada, the EU and Japan. They would negotiate first amongst themselves and then table the outcome at the GATT council. To make matters worse, the USA and Japan could never agree on most issues. The developing countries were largely bystanders.

Very soon, I found myself in the inner circle of decision-makers, which came to be called the "Green Room" process. A few months later, Dunkel resigned on account of not being able to make headway in bringing the Uruguay Round Negotiations to a close.

He was succeeded by Peter Sutherland, a former Irish Minister. Built like a rumbustious rugby player, he was not a man to be easily trifled with. He did not suffer fools. He soon got the process going with vigour after it had been stalled for seven years and in a matter of a year, the negotiations were formally concluded on 15 April 1994.[18] Peter Sutherland was hailed as the "Man of the Hour". However, he did not stay long in Geneva as other opportunities beckoned.

I also had to handle the process to select Peter's successor, Renato Ruggerio, a former Italian Trade Minister. He and I worked closely in implementing the results of the Uruguay Round.

Back to my duties in Geneva, as chairman of the Committee I had to oversee a number of agreements and obtain consensus on all decisions. It was a truly democratic system where everyone had to sign off. This required one to work with people of different countries at many levels. In short, one had to be on good terms with everyone.

I was lucky to have a group of amiable and like-minded ambassadors, including Ambassador Zutchi and Ambassador Narayanan of India, Ambassador Yerxa from the USA, Ambassador Tran and Ambassador Jean Pierre Leng from the EU, Ambassador William Rossier from Switzerland, Ambassador Wade Armstrong and Alastair Bisley from

---

[18] Sandeep Chauhan, *GATT to WTO: Gandhian Alternative to New International Economic Order* (Deep & Deep Publications, 2001) p 57.

New Zealand, Ambassador Don Kenyon from Australia and my fellow ASEAN colleagues.

I was also fortunate in the GATT secretariat to have had Arif Huesein, an experienced and skilled trade official. We worked together so smoothly that when the Uruguay negotiations were concluded, a journalist, Mr Raghavan, who represented the Third World Network, described our actions as "thieves stealing in the night". Arif and I were amused and we took it as a compliment. To be able "to steal" something from someone who had been monitoring the trade negotiations process for over 30 years was no easy feat!

Credit must also be given to my colleagues in the Mission, namely, Margaret Liang, Yong Siew Min, Tan Yee Woan, Joseph Teo, Ng Bee Kim, Rossman Ithnin, Sivasubramaniam, Peter Govindasamy, and my indispensable secretaries, Catherine Tan and Vivien. They constituted a well-oiled team which was the envy of many other missions.

A significant event that occurred during my tenure as chairman of the Council in Geneva was to oversee the entry of the People's Republic of China (PRC) and Chinese Taipei into the World Trade Organization (WTO). After 13 years of negotiations, with Swiss Ambassador Pierre Louis Girard as chair and Arif Huesein as secretary of the committee, the negotiations were finally concluded. During the lengthy negotiations, the developed countries led by the USA extracted every concession that they could get from the PRC. The process was particularly difficult as it involved a state-centred Communist economy being brought into a system based on liberalised trade and free enterprise. The Chinese leaders and their negotiating team had to experience a sharp learning curve. Finally, the deed was done and the PRC took its place as a member of the rules-based international trading community.

I had to oversee the formal entry process. The PRC negotiators demanded that their country be made a member first and Chinese Taipei be admitted thereafter. I insisted, however, that both sides be admitted simultaneously, as I did not want to run the risk of one side vetoing the entry of the other after being admitted.

The Chinese leaders and their officials in Geneva learnt the rules of the game quickly and became adept at operating under a newly created international trading system. On their part, the developed countries were satisfied that they had brought a rapidly growing economic power into the WTO fold. The developing countries were happy that their position had been strengthened by the entry of a country which would be sympathetic to their cause. The PRC's entry into the WTO, and its espousal of free trade, was to have tremendous geopolitical and economic consequences.

Upon our return from Marrakesh, Morroco, in 1995, where the Uruguay Round Agreement was formally concluded and the WTO established, I was elected the first chairman of the WTO Ministerial Council. The Council also unanimously agreed that the first meeting of the WTO Ministerial Council be held in Singapore. The work entailed implementing all the agreements signed under the aegis of the Uruguay Round and making preparations for the Ministerial meeting in Singapore.

Just as the planning for the journey to Singapore was proceeding smoothly, it was interrupted by a domestic issue that caught the attention of the world: the caning of American teenager, Michael Fay, in Singapore. He was charged in the Singapore court for vandalism and sentenced to four months in jail and six strokes of the cane.

The then US Trade Representative (USTR), Micky Kantor, took umbrage at the punishment meted out to Michael Fay and threatened to block the Ministerial meeting from taking place in Singapore. The US Permanent Representative in Geneva, Booth Gardner, tried to convince Kantor that the two issues should not be intertwined. The EU Trade Commissioner, Sir Leon Brittan, in an effort to be helpful, made a compromise suggestion that the first Ministerial Conference be held in Geneva and the second in Singapore. I held firm to the decision made by the WTO Council that the first meeting should be in Singapore.

Fortunately, I had the wholehearted support of all the other WTO delegations. On the last day of my tenure as WTO Council Chairman, I tabled a resolution on the Ministerial Conference being held in Singapore. Booth Gardner, who by then had become a personal friend, looked the other way when I gaveled the passing of the motion. His staff rushed up to him and said this was against the instructions of the USTR, but the deed was done and the Ministerial Conference was to be held in Singapore. However, the negotiations leading up to it proved to be difficult. In fact, the likely failure of the conference was staring us in the face.

The sticking point was on the future agenda of the WTO. The developed countries, and the EU in particular, wanted to add a social clause and a reference to environmental sustainability onto the agenda, as items for the next round of trade negotiations. These came to be called the "Singapore issues", and although we were the hosts, we were neutral.

The developing countries were adamant in insisting that the offers made by the developed countries in areas like textiles should be implemented before new issues could be brought onto the WTO agenda. The logjam was finally broken by the Malaysian Minister for Trade and Industry, Rafidah Aziz, who suggested that the four issues could be "discussed" in the run-up to the next round of trade negotiations. This was enough for the Singapore delegation and the WTO Secretariat to run with the ball and an agreement to that effect was swiftly formulated and adopted.

As Sandeep Chauhan puts it in his book, *GATT to WTO*:[19]

> The historical five-day ministerial conference of the WTO held in Singapore recently was a fair success, despite complaints by some member countries that they were discriminated against. The meeting's agenda was not an easy one because evolving a consensus on contentious issues like labor standard and multilateral investment and information technology was indeed

---

[19] Sandeep Chauhan, *GATT to WTO: Gandhian Alternative to New International Economic Order* (Deep & Deep Publications, 2001) p 83.

> a daunting task yet, at the end of it most of the 128 members of the nascent WTO had reason to be happy about the outcome of the meet. While the US rejoiced in its successful efforts at wrapping up the Information Technology Agreement (ITA), the European bloc was happy to have got its priorities in terms of product coverage included in the pact ... developing countries like India had to settle for some compromises on some issues, the consensus was enduring such as government procurement and the textiles agreement. Twenty-eight least developed countries complained that despite contributing less than one per cent of world trade, they were being denied effective market access by developed countries.

On the whole, the first WTO Ministerial Meeting in Singapore went off smoothly. Part of the credit goes to Ambassador Tommy Koh, who insisted that the NGOs coming to Singapore should be treated well and given access to information on the proceedings of the Conference and be briefed regularly. As a result, the Singapore Ministerial Meeting was the only Meeting to date which has not experienced demonstrations or protests by NGOs and other aggrieved parties.

Looking at the state that the WTO is in today, I cannot but feel sad that the aims and aspirations with which the organisation was set up will not be realised. With President Trump threatening to withdraw the US from the WTO, will it become another casualty in the tussle between "Fair Trade and Free Trade"?

After six years in Geneva and having completed my assignment, I was asked by then Permanent Secretary, Kishore Mahbubani, to stay on for another three years. I declined. Having completed what I had been sent to do, I wanted to leave Geneva and embark on the next phase of my diplomatic journey.

My wife left her own mark in Geneva. Some years later, when President Halimah Yacob delivered a speech at a Jamiyah function in Singapore, she said that she had known us for 40 years and she remembered Padmini as well as the dinner that we had hosted for the Singapore delegation to the International Labour Organization in Geneva. President Halimah Yacob had visited us as part of the delegation representing the National Trades Union Congress.

There are two personal achievements from my time in Geneva: one was stopping smoking in WTO meetings and the other was preventing Singapore's graduation to developed-country status. An article in *The Straits Times* by Irene Ngoo recounts how the former was done:[20]

> During the final negotiations on the Uruguay Round in 1993, when meetings dragged late into the night, the council room would be thick with cigarette smoke. Unable to bear the smoke-filled atmosphere, Mr Kesavapany started a no-smoking campaign.

---

[20] Irene Ngoo, "Man who snuffed out smoking in meeting rooms" (*The Straits Times*, 2 February 1995).

He won support quickly and, in July 1993, smoking was banned in all GATT meetings and other common areas such as the lifts and toilets.

On the issue of graduation, I was given strict instructions by Headquarters, before my departure to Geneva, that I was not to allow Singapore to be graduated. However, EU Ambassador Tran was bent on achieving the opposite. At a meeting of the committee convened to discuss this issue, Ambassador Tran tabled a formal paper. My friend and fellow golfer, Ambassador Luis Lamperia of Brazil, walked up to the table and tore up the paper! Naturally, Ambassador Tran was hopping mad. However, he could not do anything as he found no support from any of the other ambassadors. This again illustrates the value of friendship in multilateral diplomacy.

Time in Geneva was also made special by Senior Minister Lee Kuan Yew's visit to Davos. Accompanied by Mrs Lee, he found the visit enjoyable and fruitful. One secret I found out was that he would indulge in sweet things which were forbidden to him, especially when Mrs Lee was not around. On one occasion, he was to address a meeting late in the evening. Somehow, he found out that there was a Lebanese reception close by. He insisted on going to the reception despite my pleas that it would be very noisy and crowded. On arrival at the reception, Mr Lee went straight for the Lebanese sweets and indulged in them with gusto like a schoolboy. My efforts to pull him away from the dessert table were in vain.

On another occasion, when both of us were having lunch, I asked if he would like a glass of beer. He said yes. I then signalled to his staff to bring the low-alcohol Swan beer which had been lugged all the way from Australia. However, he said he would try the local brew. After one glass, he had another. The myth that he and Mrs Lee only drank beer that had low alcohol content was shattered.

The quality of our time in Geneva was enhanced by another Benji entering our lives. He was Dasho Paljor Dorji, otherwise also popularly known as Benji Dorji, the Ambassador of Bhutan to the United Nations. He became a central figure during our stay in Geneva. Selfless and generous, he easily made friends and was an effective representative for his country. When I was recovering from a broken arm after a skiing accident, Benji would come almost daily just to take me out for drives.

Through him, we came to know about the Dragon Kingdom of Bhutan and its people. Wisely ruled by King Jigme Khesar Namgyei Wangchuck, the country is known for its espousal of the "Gross Happiness Index". His Majesty's father had abdicated in favour of his son and also ensured that power was vested in the hands of the people. During our several visits there, we came to know what a special country Bhutan is. Unfortunately, the two Benjis did not see eye to eye as the former, the four-legged one, was terrified of the latter.

The Straits Times, 2 February 1995

NEW CHAIRMAN OF GENERAL COUNCIL

Man who snuffed out smoking in meeting rooms

Mr Kesavapany: Started a no-smoking campaign.

GENEVA — Trade delegates breathe easier at World Trade Organisation meetings — thanks to Singapore diplomat K. Kesavapany.

The key role he played in banning smoking in the meeting rooms of the WTO's Geneva headquarters was revealed on Tuesday by Hungarian Ambassador Andras Szepesi, a self-confessed chain-smoker.

Moving Mr Kesavapany's nomination as chairman of the first WTO general council, Mr Szepesi praised the teacher-turned-diplomat as a skilled trade negotiator and a problem solver.

He also dwelt on Mr Kesavapany's contributions to the conclusion of the Uruguay Round trade negotiations and the various key positions he held in Gatt, and praised his political skills in arriving at multilateral solutions.

To chuckles from delegates, he added that he would remember Mr Kesavapany "as the man responsible for stopping smoking in the main meeting room".

He recalled how non-smokers seated elbow-to-elbow with smokers at meetings used to suffer in silence, out of diplomacy, when they found themselves enveloped in clouds of nicotine puffs.

During the final negotiations on the Uruguay Round in 1993, when meetings dragged late into the night, the council room would be thick with cigarette smoke. Unable to bear the smoke-filled atmosphere, Mr Kesavapany started a no-smoking campaign.

He won support quickly and, in July 1993, smoking was banned in all Gatt meetings and other common areas such as the lifts and toilets.

Mr Kesavapany's nomination was seconded by Argentinian ambassador Juan Carlos Sanchez Arnau, who praised the Singapore envoy for his knowledge of international affairs and trade rules.

Indonesian Ambassador Soemadi Brotodiningrat, speaking for Asean countries, said Mr Kesavapany's candidacy was "a positive contribution of Asean to the early work of the WTO".

WTO caretaker director-general Peter Sutherland, the out-going Gatt council chairman, then declared the Singapore ambassador chairman of the new WTO council.

The two men shook hands and exchanged seats, to loud applause.

Thanking delegates, Mr Kesavapany said: "Now that you have put me in the hot seat, I can only expect your continued support and cooperation." — **Irene Ngoo.**

"Well, I guess from here on, there's no more clouding world trade issues!"

■ **More reports:** Page 4

CHAPTER 13

Returning to my Roots [21]

After the six gruelling years in Geneva, my colleagues in MFA felt that I needed a break and asked for my choice for my next posting. I indicated New Zealand. They, however, felt that the neighbouring country, Australia, would be a better fit for me. My wife and I were somewhat diffident as it meant being separated from Benji, who would have to be quarantined in Hawaii for six months.

Our quandary was resolved by news from Headquarters that my next posting would be Malaysia. Although workwise it meant going from the pot into the fire, we received the news with pleasure as it meant being closer to relatives and friends. At the same time, as any diplomat knows, working in a country's closest neighbour can be challenging and fraught with uncertainty. I was proved right.

My wife and I arrived at Subang Airport. Benji had gone ahead and was already settled in the Residence. On the way to the Residence, a motorcyclist came close to the car, and made an obscene gesture.

---

[21] This chapter is adapted from a chapter first published in Gillian Koh (ed), *The Little Nation that Can: Singapore's Foreign Relations and Diplomacy* (National University of Singapore Society, 2017) pp 47–53.

This was the first indication that bilateral relations had taken a sharp downswing.

Apparently, there was a great deal of unhappiness over Senior Minister Lee Kuan Yew's remark that Johor was not a safe place. This was in connection with Tang Liang Hong's action to flee Singapore and seek refuge in Australia. He had then visited Johor Bahru to meet friends and family from Singapore. The Malaysians took umbrage at the remarks and the Mission was summoned to Wisma Putra to receive a Third Person Note.

Matters went from bad to worse as both governments quarrelled over several issues, including the relocation of the railway station from Tanjong Pagar to Woodlands and Singapore's continued access to water from Johor under the Separation Agreement.

Several attempts to clear and put the bilateral relationship on an even keel came to nought. Instead, it spiralled down even further. The then Prime Minister Dr Mahathir was incensed that Singapore had unilaterally moved its operations from Tanjong Pagar Railway station to Woodlands. In retaliation, Dr Mahathir ordered a stoppage of the sale of sand to Singapore. Access by Singapore's military aircraft into Johor's airspace was also denied.

Action was also taken to cut off interactions at various levels, including the cessation of the games held between the Civil Services of both sides. The only activity that survived was the annual golf game between the University of Malaya and the University of Singapore Alumni. This was on account of the then Chancellor of the University of Malaya, the Yang di-Pertuan Agong, Sultan Azlan Shah's insistence that this ongoing activity should not be disrupted. An avid golfer, he looked forward to the annual games held alternatively in Malaysia and Singapore.

His counterpart, the Chancellor of NUS and President of Singapore, Mr SR Nathan, was also supportive of the games being held as scheduled. Although a non-golfer, President Nathan rode in a buggy and kept his counterpart company on the course. The social interactions that followed the games cemented the relationship between the two Heads of State.

One hilarious moment was when the Agong's golf ball was lodged in the fronds of a coconut tree. Not all the Royal commands could make the ball dislodge itself and drop to the ground! The sportsman that he was, the Agong took a penalty and dropped a new ball.

In contrast to this royal gesture of sportsmanship, the Singapore contingent to the Commonwealth Games in Kuala Lumpur was booed on entering the Stadium at Bukit Jalil. This was due to the emotions that had been whipped up to show displeasure over Singapore's refusal to settle outstanding issues. The Singapore officials and I stood ramrod straight to cheer our Singapore contingent.

Dr Mahathir's major irritation was over the fact that Singapore was continuing to pay the price of three sen per 1,000 gallons of water as stipulated in the Water Agreements. In a propaganda onslaught, Malaysian researchers were enlisted to write articles comparing the price of a hamburger with the price that Singapore was paying for the water it was receiving from Johor. According to the *Water Talks* publication published in 2003, Johor sold water to Johoreans at RM3.95 per 1,000 gallons, which it bought from Singapore at 50 sen per 1,000 gallons.

Singapore maintained its position that it was prepared to consider a revision of the price in the context of negotiation of a package of issues.

The financial crisis which hit the region in 1997 provided the opportunity for a fresh attempt to work on the package of issues. Singapore responded positively to Malaysia's request for financial assistance. In return, it sought the purchase of water on a long-term basis, with an increase in pricing. However, the failure to agree on the quantum and terms for the financial assistance to be given by Singapore to Malaysia led to a discontinuation of the negotiations on the issue. Central Limit Order Book (CLOB) was another issue which soured bilateral atmospherics.

As for water and the other outstanding issues, several attempts were made to find a comprehensive solution, including two visits to Kuala Lumpur in 2000 and 2001 by then Senior Minister Lee Kuan Yew. In a letter to SM Lee dated 21 February 2001, the Prime Minister of Malaysia, Dr Mahathir Mohamad, offered to sell raw water to Singapore at a "fair price" of 60 sen per 1,000 gallons in return for concessions on other elements of the package. Responding to the offer, and in a letter dated 23 April 2001, SM Lee said that although there were some elements to be resolved on the water issue, if there was "give and take on both sides, an agreement is possible". In this spirit,

SM Lee undertook his second visit to Kuala Lumpur in September 2001.

While the negotiations were in progress, the Malaysian government, inexplicably, raised the asking price to RM3 per 1,000 gallons, making it 100 times more than the existing price of raw water. This amount was subsequently raised to RM6.25. Such increases made it difficult for common ground to be reached and led to a stalemate in the negotiations.

In the meantime, efforts by Singapore to increase its local supply of water began to bear fruit. Besides water imported from Malaysia, it moved towards self-sufficiency in its water requirements by obtaining water from four sources: imported water from Malaysia; desalination; recycling used water (NEWater); and water from local catchments (such as stormwater runoff and reservoirs). These measures, known as the Four National Taps strategy, led to the water issue, which had hitherto been a flash point in the bilateral relationship, being relegated to the background. Future talks on this issue would be on the basis of a "willing seller, willing buyer". Singapore has indicated that it would not seek a renewal of the 1961 Water Agreement, which expired in 2011. Thereafter, the 1962 Water Agreement will continue to be in force until 2061.

An issue that threatened to rile bilateral relations was the Malaysian allegation that Singapore had encroached into Malaysian waters when it had undertaken reclamation works. Professor Tommy Koh, who was the agent in this case and later in the Pedra Branca case, said (in an email communication with me dated 26 December 2018):

> Malaysia had objected to our land reclamation activities in Pualu Tekong and Tuas. Malaysia alleged that we had intruded into their waters, caused irreparable harm to their marine environment. Malaysia unilaterally initiated arbitrary proceedings against Singapore and then applied to the International Tribunal for the Law of the Sea, in Hamburg, for provisional measures.
>
> The tribunal rejected Malaysia's application and instructed the two governments to establish a group of independent experts to verify the facts. A year later, they submitted a unanimous report. Based on that report, the two governments were able to arrive at an amicable settlement.

The joint statement issued on that occasion revealed a decided consciousness to resolve problems in an atmosphere of goodwill. An excerpt from the statement reads as follows:[22]

> The positive outcome of the meeting between Malaysia and Singapore delegations reflects the goodwill and cooperation which exist between them and their respective governments. This augurs well for the further strengthening of good relations between the two friendly close neighbours.

The amicable manner in which the land reclamation issue was settled gave rise to hopes that the dispute over Pedra Branca could be similarly settled. Both countries agreed to submit the dispute over

---

[22] Singapore Government press release, 9 January 2005: "Case Concerning Land Reclamation by Singapore in and around the Straits of Johor (Malaysia v Singapore)" <http://www.nas.gov.sg/archivesonline/speeches/view-html?filename=2005011402.htm>

Pedra Branca, Middle Rocks and South Ledge, to the International Court of Justice (ICJ). After a process that lasted 14 years, the court delivered its judgment as follows:[23]

- "Sovereignty of the Pedra Branca – Pulau Batu Puteh belongs to the Republic of Singapore."
- "Sovereignty over Middle Rocks belongs to Malaysia."
- "Sovereignty over South Ledge belongs to the State in the territorial waters of which it is located."

Although the split judgment of the court did not completely satisfy both countries, it was accepted with equanimity and grace.

However, in 2017, the Najib government applied to the ICJ to revise and interpret the 2008 judgment. The Mahathir government discontinued both applications when it came to power in May 2018.

Yet another issue that emerged in 2001 to roil the waters was Malaysia's move to demolish the Causeway and replace it with a bridge. Among the reasons cited for this action was that the bridge was essential for free flow of water through the Straits. Singapore was not convinced by the reason given. Digging in his heels, Dr Mahathir announced that Malaysia would build a "crooked bridge" on its side of the Causeway. Before any action could be taken on the matter, Dr Mahathir resigned from the post of Prime Minister, after 22 years in office.

---

[23] S Jayakumar & Tommy Koh, *Pedra Branca: The Road to the World Court* (NUS Press, 2009) pp 161–190.

Personally, I was happy that Abdullah Badawi, a long-term Foreign Minister of Malaysia, would succeed Dr Mahathir as Prime Minister. A kind-hearted gentleman, he put emphasis on improving ties with Singapore as a priority. One indication of his close relationship with Singapore leaders was the invitation extended to Ministers Wong Kan Seng and Prof Jayakumar to his daughter's wedding. No other foreign guests had been invited. The next day, Pak Lah, as he was popularly called, entertained both the ministers to a game of golf and took them home for tea. I was also a beneficiary of this warm expression of friendship.

Prime Minister Abdullah Badawi felt there were some "low-hanging" fruits that could be plucked. However, the decision not to proceed with the "crooked bridge" project earned him the enmity of Dr Mahathir. He also did not have the political clout to ensure that the agreements reached with Singapore on the sale of sand and airspace issues could be made to stick.

As in the case of Geneva, I had an excellent team to work with in Kuala Lumpur: Vanu Gopala Menon (currently High Commissioner in Kuala Lumpur), Peter Tan (now Deputy Secretary at Headquarters), Stanley Loh (now Ambassador to China), Chin Hock Seng (who left MFA to undertake missionary work), Kamal Vaswani, Sam Tan, Adrian Tan and Mark Neo. Of course, Sylvia Toh was my indispensable Personal Assistant. Returning to Singapore, I continue to keep an eye on developments across the Causeway and on the state of bilateral relations.

I cannot end my Foreign Service career without paying respect to the succession of Singapore foreign ministers who have helped to craft and shape the country's foreign policy, namely Mr S Rajaratnam, Mr S Dhanabalan, Mr Wong Kan Seng, Professor S Jayakumar, Mr George Yeo and Mr K Shanmugam. Although I did not serve with Dr Vivian Balakrishnan, I had the pleasure of interacting with him when he visited Malaysia and on other occasions.

Likewise, Singapore was well-served by a number of high calibre Permanent Secretaries who provided the ballast to keep Singapore's foreign relations strong and sturdy. Of course, when it came to Malaysia, Mr Lee Kuan Yew himself was the "Foreign Minister and CEO".

Upon Abdullah Badawi's stepping down, Najib Razak took over as Prime Minister. Like Abdullah Badawi, Najib felt that a cooperative rather than confrontational approach in dealing with Singapore could yield results. With the railway issue resolved, most of the bilateral problems that had bedevilled ties between the two countries were put to bed. This enabled both governments to look at positive avenues for cooperation, including the construction of a fast speed rail link (High-Speed Railway) from Singapore to Kuala Lumpur. Both sides also explored win-win partnerships through the joint venture projects. Action was also taken to look at cooperation in other areas such as environmental sustainability, religious extremism and drug related issues.

However, the unexpected outcome of the 14th General Elections in Malaysia held on 9 May 2018 led to tumultuous changes in Malaysia. The Barisan National, which had been in power for over 60 years, suffered massive losses and in its place, Pakatan Harapan (PH) became the new government with Dr Mahathir returning as Prime Minister. Soon, some of the old bilateral issues began to resurface.

Dr Mahathir lost no little time in bringing up the issue of water pricing. Speaking to a Channel NewsAsia reporter, Sumisha Naidu, Dr Mahathir described the 3 sen per 1,000 gallons of raw water that Malaysia sold to Singapore under the 1962 Water Agreement as "ridiculous". Several of his Cabinet colleagues and the Mentri Besar of Johor joined in the call for Singapore to pay a higher water price.

Singapore's Minister for Foreign Affairs, Dr Vivian Balakrishnan, reiterated Singapore's longstanding position that Malaysia had lost the right to review the price of water and that neither Malaysia nor Singapore can unilaterally change the terms of the 1962 Water Agreement.

On 25 July 2018, the Malaysian Minister for Foreign Affairs, Dato Saifuddin Abdullah, said that "it is definitely not in our minds to turn off taps". What his country sought, he said, was to renegotiate the pricing. It remains to be seen how this issue will evolve in the coming months and years.

Yet another issue emerged within one month of PH taking office. Prime Minister Mahathir announced that in order to contain the debt incurred by the Najib government, the High-Speed Rail (HSR) project would be cancelled. Subsequently, it was announced that the HSR project would be suspended. The issue of the crooked bridge has also resurfaced, with Malaysian ministers putting forward their own versions of what this bridge should be.

THE BUSINESS TIMES, **FEBRUARY 7 2004**

THE DIPLOMAT'S DIPLOMAT

Director of the Institute of South-east Asian Studies, past chairman of the WTO General Council, and chief negotiator for Singapore's 'bilaterals'. With all that on his plate, K Kesavapany's 'people skills' certainly come in handy, as **VIKRAM KHANNA** finds out

A HISTORIAN by background, he wasn't even an economist, much less a trade specialist. Yet in 1994, K Kesavapany was able to rise to the highest echelons in the world of international trade diplomacy: he became chairman of the General Council (the governing body) of the World Trade Organisation (WTO) - and made a success of it.

Soft-spoken, informal, accessible and disarmingly modest, 'Pany' as he is called (including by himself; he even signs off his emails with his nickname) had the one qualification that really counts in the delicate, high-stakes world of international diplomacy: the ability to, as he puts it, 'get people together'.

That skill also proved valuable when he served as Singapore's High Commissioner to Malaysia from 1996 to 2003 - a particularly turbulent period in bilateral relations.

Pany is quick to point out that it wasn't just his 'people skills' that landed him the WTO job - which he got with the unanimous approval of his fellow ambassadors. It was also Singapore's unique position in international trade.

'Singapore has always been a member of the green room', a group of about 18-20 key trade ambassadors who help the director-general of the WTO in moving trade negotiations forward,' he says, sitting in his office at the Institute of South-east Asian Studies, of which he is now the director.

'Singapore is also seen as a neutral country on trade. We belong to the NIEs (newly industrialising economies), but we still are part of the developing world. We are part of Asean, but we are free traders and pro-liberalisation. So everybody thought I was the safe candidate. The job requirement was to be friendly, sincere, open to all members; to be seen as not having a hidden agenda and not speaking on behalf of one group or another.'

This ability to smooth feathers, be seen as fair and even-handed and keep a boat full of edgy trade ministers from rocking, is worth its weight in gold in a place like the WTO, where consensus means everything. As Pany explains: 'Even one chap from the general council can stand up out of 130 members and just say I object' and then you're stuck. You can't move, until the guy changes his mind.'

As chair of the WTO's general council, Pany followed a couple of golden rules of diplomacy, which helped ensure that trade negotiations moved forward and didn't get bogged down. 'One thing I made very sure: never put on the table any issue on which members privately cannot agree,' he says.

'In other words, you carry out consultations privately. And unless and until you have managed to get almost everyone on board, you don't table something for discussion. That way, everybody feels they have been consulted and their interests have been taken into account. It made people feel comfortable and reassured that I wouldn't pull a fast one.'

Golden rule number two: 'You cultivate people - not when you need them, but over a period of time. A lot of trade relations depend on personal relationships. If someone doesn't like you, he has nothing to lose by opposing you. On the other hand, there have been instances when the trade ambassadors on the spot have taken decisions contrary to instructions from their capitals. They have then worked backwards, getting back to their capitals to explain.'

Today, however, international trade relations have become fraught with conflict. The so-called 'Doha Round' of multilateral trade talks - which followed the Uruguay Round - are stalemated, and all attempts at breakthroughs (the latest being at Cancun, Mexico, late last year) have failed.

Pany is circumspect about the prospects. 'The tragedy of the WTO today is that it has become a battleground between the developed and developing countries. Issues are no longer being looked at on the basis of their merits. An element of ideology has crept in. There is an ideological debate between the rich countries - the so-called North - and the poorer countries of the South.

'This is largely because a lot of past promises have not been kept, on both sides. For instance, the rich countries said they'll open up textiles, but that hasn't happened. Nor have they cut their agricultural subsidies. On the other hand, the developing countries haven't opened up. Both sides are guilty.

'The tragedy is that the differences are so sharp that it has become very difficult to bridge the gap. For example, when I was in Geneva, two months ago, there was an attempt to resume the dialogue. One ambassador just got up and said, Don't bother to put any text on the table, we'll just reject it out of hand.' Of course, extraneous global events like Sept 11 and the response may be influencing things - or the notion that the US is acting unilaterally. Because the WTO doesn't operate in isolation, it operates in a world context.'

But Pany remains hopeful. 'I know things look difficult at this point,' he says. 'But those of us who have been involved in trade negotiations, we know: ultimately people come around. The Tokyo Round (which preceded the Uruguay Round of trade talks) took about 10 years, the Uruguay Round took eight years. So it's a cycle. People have to get their angst out.

Meanwhile, Pany is busy helping with the negotiation of Singapore's still-expanding network of bilateral free-trade agreements (FTAs), having been particularly active in the Korea-Singapore FTA. Although an avowed 'multilateralist', he passionately defends Singapore's 'bilaterals'.

'I have always been a multilateralist,' he says. 'But when the multilateral system is at an impasse, you have to look at other avenues. What we're looking at through these bilaterals is strike in WTO-plus' agreements. That is, what issues cannot be negotiated multilaterally, we're negotiating bilaterally - for example, investment, competition policy and mutual recognition of standards.'

In defence of bilaterals

But trade purists have pointed out that Singapore's bilaterals - like any bilaterals - are discriminatory in nature and violate the fundamental principle of multilateralism, namely, the 'most-favoured-nation' principle, which states that any trade concession made to one country should be extended to all others.

'Yes, but what is happening is that the waves are spreading,' says Pany. 'We started off with New Zealand. Now we're working to expand that agreement to include Chile. Japan has come in, Australia has come in, the US has come in, Korea has come in. And India has come in. India, which is not prepared to talk about investment at the WTO, is prepared to talk about it at a bilateral level. So sooner or later, all these agreements can be hoisted on to the WTO. There'll be a lattice of agreements. And countries will find there's nothing wrong with talking about investment, competition policy, trade facilitation.

'Two more points. One, we are compatible with Article 24 of WTO, which says we must cover a substantial part of trade - and we've done that with all our agreements. Second, we want to pursue a path where the WTO can go in the future. Right now, some developing countries are unable to liberalise fast, but others are able to do so.

'For example in Asean. Those countries that can move forward should do so at a faster pace than others. That doesn't mean we're ignoring the others, but those countries that are comfortable moving ahead should move ahead.'

Pany notes that countries in the region are all coming around to the idea that bilateral FTAs have their place.

'A classic example is Malaysia,' he points out. 'Malaysia used to be dead against FTAs It once held the view that Singapore was being used as a Trojan horse, that it would provide other countries with a backdoor into Asean and all that. But then the Malaysians realised they'd better join the game too. So now they're working on an FTA with Japan they want one with Korea - and with the US.

'So, if for example Singapore had said OK we will worry about what our neighbours say and not go ahead with FTAs, and the WTO is not moving and regional integration is not moving, we'd just be stuck. So we thought, so long as we don't damage either the regional integration process or the multilateral process, it's legitimate to do something that will keep the trade momentum going forward.'

CHAPTER 14

Entering the World of Academia

Returning from Malaysia in 2002, I wondered what the next phase of my life was going to be. Unknown to me, the late Mr SR Nathan and the then Permanent Secretary of MFA, Mr Chia Cheong Fook, were looking for a successor to Professor Chia Siow Yue, the Director of the Institute of Southeast Asian Studies (ISEAS).

In the belief that I could do it, they asked me to take on the job. I was rather diffident because I had no experience in the academic world. I was also not sure how the academic staff would accept the idea of a non-academic, especially a civil servant, taking on the job. There were fears that academic integrity would be compromised. However, with the backing of Mr Nathan and Mr Chia, I went to ISEAS. My entry into ISEAS was made pleasurable by the fact that the chairman of the Board of Directors was going to be none other than Professor Wang Gungwu, who hailed from the same school in Ipoh, and had also taught me at the University of Malaya in Kuala Lumpur. Professor Wang proved to be a most supportive chairman and an excellent friend. He offered his collection of books on Southeast Asia to ISEAS, which I used to set up the Wang Gungwu collection at ISEAS. Over the next ten years, I had a fruitful time in heading an institute which was the brainchild of Dr Goh Keng Swee, who felt that such an institute would foster scholarship within the region. I left the post in February 2012.

Over the ten years that I was at ISEAS, two centres were set up, namely, the ASEAN Study Centre (ASC) and the Nalanda Sriwijaya Centre (NSC). Two research units were also set up: the Archeology Unit and the Energy Studies Programme.

The ASC was set up at the request of Singapore's MFA to mark the 50th anniversary of ASEAN. The goal was to have an independent platform to comment critically on ASEAN-related matters. The ASC was fortunate in having an experienced Filipino diplomat and a former ASEAN Secretary General, Rodolfo Severino, as its Head. When I retired, Rodolfo described my time at ISEAS:[24]

> He has kept ISEAS focused on South East Asia, without necessarily projecting any one country's point of view. He has also encouraged ISEAS to break new ground on Southeast Asian affairs, such as archaeology and ancient influences on the region's diverse cultures.

Commending the initiative to set up ASC, the then ASEAN Secretary General, Surin Pitsuwan, said that the scholars working in the Centre should make their views known without fear or favour. This, he said,

---

[24] *Dear Mr Pany* (Institute of Southeast Asian Studies, 2012).

was something that those working in the Secretariat could not do as they were seconded by their respective governments. Among the outstanding scholars that the Centre has produced is Dr Sanchita Basu Das and Dr Moe Thu Zar. Dr Basu Das has moved on to become the Director of the South East Asian Region in the World Bank's Manila office. Dr Moe is well-known for her commentaries on current regional issues.

The Nalanda Sriwijaya Centre was headed by Associate Professor Tansen Sen and the Archeology Unit by Associate Professor John Miksic. All of them contributed to the furthering of ISEAS' reputation as the lead organisation for intellectual research.

As stated in the ISEAS publication *Light on a Hill,*[25]

> the idea for the revival (of Nalanda University) was mooted by then Indian President Abdul Kalam during his state visit to Singapore in 2006. It was strongly supported by then Foreign Minister George Yeo and the Buddhist Lodge. It also enjoyed the backing of the East Asia Summit (EAS), a forum for the leaders of eighteen countries in the Asia-Pacific region.

Mindful that Buddhism played an important role in connecting the countries of Asia both in historical and contemporary terms, I was amenable to the suggestion.

---

[25] Cassandra Chew, *Light on a Hill: The ISEAS – Yusof Ishak Institute Story 1968–2018* (ISEAS – Yusof Ishak Institute, 2018) p 156.

With the help of Mr Nathan, we were able to obtain a donation of $1 million from the Singapore Buddhist Lodge for the Centre. There is an interesting story of how we obtained the donation. Prior to approaching the Head of the Buddhist Lodge, Mr Lee Bock Guan, Mr Nathan took some time to produce a calligraphic scroll. I am not sure what was on the scroll. It must have been well-wishes for the Buddhist Lodge. Taking the scroll with us, we met Mr Lee, who was touched by the gesture and the thought that went into the gift. Receiving the scroll, Mr Lee asked, "How much donation are you expecting?"

I nudged Mr Nathan to ask for $1 million. Mr Lee was clearly surprised as he asked, "Only one million?" While handing over the donation, Mr Lee commented that as the proposed Buddhist Centre would be doing the noble work of promoting Buddhist studies, it was only appropriate that the Buddhist Lodge gave as much help as it could. The Buddhist Lodge made further contribution in subsequent years.

However, the then Singapore Foreign Minister, George Yeo, felt that the Centre should have wider research coverage and the name Nalanda Sriwijaya was therefore adopted. Nalanda was the name of the university built in the 9th century in Bihar, India, while Sriwijaya was the Sriwijaya Empire which flourished in the southern part of the Archipelago. The aim of the Centre was to study issues of ancient and contemporary relevance to the region. ISEAS was fortunate in getting Professor Tansen Sen, from the City University of New York, as its first Head. Professor Tansen was able to secure secondment to ISEAS for a period of three years. Under his leadership, the Centre became known in the region for its high standard of scholarship and breadth of research work. Among its notable scholars was Dr Jeffrey Wade, a specialist in Chinese history.

The establishment of the Centre coincided with the revival of the ancient Nalanda University. This was a brainchild of Minister George Yeo and Nobel Laureate Amartya Sen. The revived university was meant to serve as a regional connection between India and the rest of Asia, in the context of the East Asia Summit. Recognising the valuable work coming out of the Nalanda Sriwijaya Centre, the Board of Nalanda University accorded it the status of a "Centre of Excellence". The other such centre was at Chulalongkorn University. In Professor Tansen Sen's words (in his email communication with me dated 18 December 2018):

> The Institute of Southeast Asian Studies was the best place in Singapore to house the Nalanda Sriwijaya Centre. The key objective of the Centre was to understand the intricacies of intra-Asian interactions focused on the role and contribution of Southeast Asia. Between 2009 and 2012, the Centre started transforming the field of intra-Asian studies through conferences, publications, visiting fellows programs, and cultural events. It attracted academics, government officials, and the general public. ISEAS emerged as a lively and energetic place for interactions of ideas and views, public engagement, and a hub for international networking. These were the many reasons for me to frequently travel between New York and Singapore. ISEAS was a place to be among fellow researchers, friends, and mentors.

Sadly, Nalanda University has not lived up to its initial promise. As stated in the book *Light on a Hill:*[26]

> Unfortunately, NSC's role in Nalanda has since been affected by the controversy over autonomy and managerial issues in the university that led to the resignation of Mr Yeo as its Chancellor and Professor Wang from its governing board in 2016.

I feel that India has lost an opportunity to project its soft power throughout the region and beyond. Like the Chinese initiative of "One road, one belt", India could also have built a Cultural Belt and taken advantage of the rich Indic heritage stretching from Myanmar to Indonesia and Cambodia. A sense of what was missed is reflected in Sahana Singh's book, *The Educational Heritage of Ancient India.*[27] Could this not have been a case of "paradise lost – paradise regained"?

The setting up of the Archeology Unit was a personal initiative of mine. I wondered why, unlike other ASEAN countries, Singapore did not have a place to study archeology. The answer given to me was that in our 200-year-old history, there was not much of archeology to study. However, a book entitled *Singapore, A 700-Year History,*[28] has shown that Singapore had a history before Raffles. The ISEAS

---

[26] Cassandra Chew, *Light on a Hill: The ISEAS – Yusof Ishak Institute Story 1968–2018* (ISEAS – Yusof Ishak Institute, 2018) p 156.

[27] Sahana Singh, *The Educational Heritage of Ancient India: How an Ecosystem of Learning Was Laid to Waste* (Notion Press, 2017) pp 9–10.

[28] Kwa Chong Guan, Derek Heng & Tan Tai Yong, *Singapore, A 700-Year History: from early emporium to world city* (National Archives of Singapore, 2009).

Board approved an allocation of $1 million for the setting up of the centre. We were fortunate to have had with us Associate Professor John Miksic to head the Unit. We were also fortunate to have had a local archeologist, Lim Chen Sian, who came on board. Together, they built up the Archeology Unit, which has since established itself as a centre for regional archeological studies.

As Associate Professor John Miksic recalled:[29]

> I was amazed when I was informed by Prof. Goh Beng Lan, head of the Department of Southeast Asian Studies at NUS, that ISEAS was interested in forming an Archaeology Unit. I had been involved with ISEAS for over 20 years. When ISEAS moved to its present site, I was invited together with Pat Lim to participate in the design of the decorations for the wall at the entrance to the Kernial Singh Sandhu Seminar Room. I felt this was a great opportunity to emphasize the ancient roots of Southeast Asian cultures, including art forms and aesthetic values that they shared as well as local originality and links with China and India. No further archaeological collaboration with ISEAS was initiated, however. ISEAS was experiencing a period during which the Institute's long-standing expertise in Southeast Asian history was being superseded by a strong focus on the prediction of future trends.

---

[29] From an email sent by Professor John Miksic to Kesavapany on 2 December 2016.

ISEAS was not alone in this. Until the formation of the NSC Archaeology Unit, there had never been any formally-sanctioned body devoted to archaeology in Singapore. I had long despaired that such an event would ever come to pass. When the NSC was formed, I was very happy, but I assumed that the scope of that organization would be restricted to history and Buddhist subjects. I had long advocated that Singapore should leverage its position as a small neutral nation to set up a centre for archaeological research and training. In conversations with many friends in ASEAN and SEAMEO over the years, I had been told over and over by representatives of many countries that Singapore was the natural site for such a centre, because it would be seen as a fair mediator between the major countries of the region, each of which has spectacular ruins and other archaeological remains. I had long given up on the prospect that such a centre would emerge. As I discussed the shape of the proposed Archaeology Unit with Ambassador Kesavapany and the NSC's director, Tansen Sen, I was overjoyed to see how closely our vision for the unit coincided. The unit would have funds for field work, publication, student training, and laboratory analysis. Though the NSC would not grant degrees, it would be able to provide academic credit for students from overseas universities.

Thus it was that the opening of the AU with President S.R. Nathan as the guest of honour was one of the happiest days of my life. The AU continues to develop after Ambassador Kesavapany, Prof. Tansen Sen, and I have moved on to other projects. I look back on the time I spent with Ambassador Kesavapany and Tansen as one

> of the happiest and most fulfilling periods of my life. If my work is to leave any legacy for future generations of archaeologists of Singapore and Southeast Asia, the AU may well be one of its most long-lasting results.

The Energy Studies Unit at ISEAS was a response to the oil crisis in 2008 and 2009. As a major oil refining and transshipment centre, oil makes a vital contribution to Singapore's economy. Recognising the need for more information and analytical studies, I asked my former MFA colleague, Mark Hong, to set up an Energy Studies Programme. The programme became very successful, with high attendance at all the talks and seminars organised by the Unit. Watching this, MFA and the Ministry of Trade asked me whether I could help to set up an energy studies centre at ISEAS. My reply was that the subject was too important and too weighty for ISEAS to handle. Besides, ISEAS could not pay for the cost of hiring energy economists, who were in great demand. Subsequently, a separate Energy Studies Institute was established and located next to ISEAS at NUS.

On the two occasions I attended the United Nations Assembly sessions in New York, I was assigned by Ambassador Tommy Koh and Ambassador Kishore Mahbubani to cover the Third Committee proceedings. This Committee deals with socio-cultural issues, including those related to gender.

It should therefore come as no surprise that at ISEAS, a Gender Studies Programme was set up during my tenure. The programme was welcomed by my friends in AWARE and in academia. Headed by social activist Braema Mathi and later by Dr Theresa Devasahayam, the programme provided a platform to study a largely neglected area. It brought together academics and civil society members in Singapore and the ASEAN region.

Gradually, the attitude towards gender studies is changing. As Professor Lee Na-Yang of Chung-Ang University said, "People used to think women studies is something like home economics, but now, many students come to class and say 'I'm a feminist'."[30]

It is gratifying that ISEAS promoted this cause.

The greatest sense of accomplishment during these ten years as the Head of ISEAS was the production of close to 100 publications, on a wide range of topics. My friend and mentor, Professor Tommy Koh, paid me a gracious compliment by saying, "You gave us some very fine books to read during your time in ISEAS."

The prominent titles from the Centre include *A Biography of S Rajaratnam* by Irene Ng,[31] *Zubir Said, the Composer of Majulah Singapura* by his daughter, Rohana Zubir,[32] *How Asia Can Shape the*

---

[30] Chang May Choon, "South Korean Feminist novel a best seller as women defy norms " (*The Straits Times*, 16 December 2018) <https://www.straitstimes.com/asia/east-asia/south-korean-feminist-novel-a-best-seller-as-women-defy-norms>

[31] Irene Ng, *The Singapore Lion: A Biography of S Rajaratnam* (Institute of Southeast Asian Studies, 2010).

[32] Rohana Zubir, *Zubir Said: The Composer of Majulah Singapura* (Institute of Southeast Asian Studies, 2012).

World by Joergen Oerstroem Moeller,[33] and *In Lieu of Ideology: An Intellectual Biography of Goh Keng Swee* by Ooi Kee Beng.[34]

My favourite of all these books, published during my time at ISEAS, was *The Dancing Girl*,[35] written by the late Dr S Balaji Sadasivan. It was based on his research of ancient and historic India. This came as a surprise to many people, including Minister Mentor Lee Kuan Yew, who wondered how a neurosurgeon could have written this book.

As the story goes, one day the Head of Publications, Triena Ong, came to see me and said that Senior Minister of State for Foreign Affairs, Dr S Balaji Sadasivan, wanted the manuscript he had written to be edited. However, it was to be published posthumously. It was an unusual request. It was only later that we found out Dr Balaji was battling cancer and knew that he did not have much time left. Triena and I went to see him in the hospital and persuaded him to let us publish his book while he was still with us. He reluctantly agreed. Triena and the staff in the Publications Department fast-tracked the production of the book. Unfortunately, Dr Balaji passed away two months before work could be completed on the book. His widow, Dr Ma Swan Hoo, stepped in and worked with us to complete the final phase of the book. Dr Ma is a medical doctor by profession, but she is passionately engaged in the promotion of the arts. She is also

---

[34] Ooi Kee Beng, *In Lieu of Ideology: An Intellectual Biography of Goh Keng Swee* (Institute of Southeast Asian Studies, 2010).

[35] Balaji Sadasivan, *The Dancing Girl: A History of Early India* (Institute of Southeast Asian Studies, 2011).

involved as a Docent in several museums, including the National Museum and the Indian Heritage Centre. She suggested the "Dancing Girl" as the title for the book. The name is based on a small figurine found in the ruins of the Harapa-Mohendajoro Civilization, which existed before the 1st century BC. It symbolises the history of the period discussed in the book. A much sought-after book of this genre, it is being republished and will be presented at the Indian Heritage Centre shortly.

One of the books I wanted to commission was a biography of the then Prime Minister Goh Chok Tong. I felt that Singaporeans needed to know how he managed the political transition from the first generation to the second generation of leaders. When I approached him at a lunch he had hosted at the Istana, he said "nothing grows under the oak tree". I am glad that a book on him has since been published, titled *Tall Order* by Peh Shing Huei.[36] This book makes for essential reading for those who want to know about the life and times of Singapore's second Prime Minister.

Yet another book, *Sarsikyo: Woven Buddhist Ribbons of Myanmar* which was commissioned by ISEAS, was written by a visiting Research Fellow, Vanessa Chan.[37] She undertook research on a particular textile that can only be found in Myanmar. In the course of her research, Vanessa came across one of the last two or three people

---

[36] Peh Shing Huei, *Tall Order – The Goh Chok Tong Story* (World Scientific Publishing, 2018).

[37] Vanessa Chan, *Sarsikyo: Woven Buddhist Ribbons of Myanmar* (ISEAS-Yusof Ishak Institute, Nalanda-Sriwijaya Centre Working Paper No 29, December 2018).

left in the country who actually knew how to make this textile. She turned the research project into a social enterprise which has helped to revive the art and brought it back into the market. Expressing her thanks, Vanessa, who is now Singapore's Ambassador to Myanmar, said (in an email communication with me dated 9 January 2019), "So you and NSC have also helped to resurrect a traditional craft from extinction!" This is an example of how a research institute can help society to unearth hidden treasures.

One of the prominent visitors to ISEAS during my time was Her Royal Highness Princess Maha Chakri Sirindhorn of the Kingdom of Thailand. A highly regarded scholar, Her Royal Highness consented to the Board's invitation to be the first ISEAS Distinguished Honorary Fellow in 2012.

Another prominent visitor was the Harvard-trained scholar-prince, Raja Nazrin of Perak, Malaysia. Raja Nazrin would make unannounced visits to the ISEAS bookshop to browse through and purchase our publications. On one of these visits, the staff alerted me to the presence of His Royal Highness. I went to meet him right away and it was the beginning of a friendship. Now the Sultan of Perak, Tuanku continues to be known for his sagacity and wise leadership.

Yet another famous personality to visit ISEAS was the late Chin Peng, the long-time leader of the Malayan Communist Party in the 1940s and 1950s. A determined and committed anti-colonialist, he led the party's guerilla insurgency during the Malayan Emergency. As he was banned from entering Malaysia and Singapore, it was nothing short of a James Bond type of adventure to bring him into Singapore for a talk. When he walked into ISEAS, I was half-expecting a thin and weathered guerilla fighter. Instead, I met a portly businessman figure. Chin Peng gave a compelling talk at ISEAS, in 2004, to a full house, though with an acute touch of amnesia. He also had a one-on-one meeting with Minister Mentor Lee Kuan Yew. How I wish I had been a fly on the wall at that meeting. He also visited his old hunting ground in Queen Street. Chin Peng's wish to return to the place where he was born, Sitiawan, Perak, did not materialise as the Malaysian government denied him entry. He died in 2013, far away from the land where he was born.

Looking back, I had a wonderful group of colleagues to work with at ISEAS, too many to mention by name individually. Special mention, however, must be made of my PA, Christina Goh. She was a secretary, mother and confidant all rolled into one. She was especially fond of Padmini and our friendship continues until today.

As a farewell present, my colleagues presented me with a book entitled *Dear Mr Pany*,[38] comprising of a collection of individual comments and notes. This book remains the most treasured item on my bookshelf.

During the period when I was at ISEAS, I was also Singapore's Non-Resident Ambassador to Jordan. It was an interesting and eventful assignment.

---

[38] *Dear Mr Pany* (Institute of Southeast Asian Studies, 2012).

However, even before this, I was already acquainted with Jordan by virtue of having chaired a working group which dealt with the process of admitting Jordan into WTO. For this, I was honoured with the title "The Order of Independence First Class by the Hashemite Kingdom of Jordan" in 2000. Due to this experience, I was already known to high-ranking Jordanian officials. Jordan and Singapore enjoy the most cordial of relations. King Abdullah openly expresses his admiration for Singapore's achievements and calls on his ministers and civil servants to view Singapore as a model for development.

One of the wishes of any Ambassador is to be able to welcome his Head of State to the country of his posting. This wish was fulfilled when President Nathan and Mrs Umi Nathan visited Jordan. They were warmly welcomed by King Abdullah and Queen Rania. It was during this trip that President Nathan also signed a petition to make Petra a World Heritage site. The delegation also visited the ancient and historic sites of Jordan, including Petra. Both Heads of State inaugurated the Jordan-Singapore Vocational Training Centre at Marka. The Centre was aimed at training technicians for the region. Several years later, the Centre was handed over to the Jordanians to run.

One personal achievement was to persuade the Jordanian government to give equal treatment, in terms of fee payment, to Singapore students studying in Jordan. There were less than ten Singapore students in Jordan at that point in time. Now, I am told, there are 168 students pursuing degrees in Islamic Jurisprudence and other subjects. Mr and Mrs Nathan were welcomed by the students during the State Visit.

My tour of duty in Jordan was made pleasurable and fruitful by the friendship and goodwill extended by our Honorary Consul-General George Emile Ibrahim Haddad and his wife, Sherin. George, a well-known businessman, is very committed to developing ties between Singapore and Jordan. His wife, Sherin, is equally engaged in building ties between our countries. Both of them have become "family". George was given the Public Service Star National Day Award by the Singapore government in 2016 for services rendered.

Another Jordanian friend was Bassem Abadalah, a former minister. Every time I went to Jordan, he would host lunch at his residence and invite his friends in high places. Over lunch, they would discuss a variety of issues pertaining to domestic and foreign matters. I was privileged to sit in and listen to their conversations.

After a period of ten happy and wonderful years, as Non-Resident Ambassador to Jordan, I was happy to hand over duties to my successor, Mr Shamsher Zamen, a businessman with wide trading connections in the region. He was an admirable choice to further relations between Singapore and Jordan. I am also glad that the Hashemite Kingdom of Jordan has opened a full embassy in Singapore with His Excellency Mahmoud Daifallah Hmoud as the Ambassador.

I will always cherish my appointment as Non-Resident Ambassador to Jordan and regard it as one of the high points of my diplomatic career.

world.*regional*

The Straits Times, 27 November 2010

Iseas director gets top award from Cambodia

By Rachel Lin

AMBASSADOR K. Kesavapany, director of the Institute of Southeast Asian Studies (Iseas), has been conferred Cambodia's top national award reserved for foreigners.

He received the Royal Order of Sahametrei, Commander rank, from Cambodian Deputy Prime Minister Sok An in Phnom Penh yesterday evening.

Mr Kesavapany was in the Cambodian capital to address the Royal Academy of Cambodia on the topic, The Challenge For Asean In The 21st Century.

The award recognised his work in organising a Cambodia Forum in Singapore in April.

The forum was held jointly by Iseas and the Cambodian Institute for Cooperation and Peace. During the forum, Dr Sok An had led a delegation to Singapore and met Prime Minister Lee Hsien Loong.

The delegation had also visited Iseas and was "very impressed" by the organisation, Mr Kesavapany said.

A statement from the Cambodian Office of the Council of Ministers said the forum had attracted many national and international experts.

"The forum is crucially important and relevant for the development of Cambodia," it added.

At the award ceremony, Dr Sok An, speaking in Khmer, praised Iseas as a reputable, well-known institution that furthered the Asean cause.

Mr Kesavapany said he was honoured to receive the award.

Mr Kesavapany (right) and Dr Sok An at the award ceremony in Phnom Penh yesterday. The Iseas director was lauded for his work in organising a Cambodia Forum in Singapore in April. PHOTO: ISEAS

"More than that, its significance is in recognising Iseas for promoting Cambodia-Singapore relations as well as interest in Asean," he added.

Mr Pou Sothirak, the former Cambodian ambassador to Japan, said the Royal Academy of Cambodia and Iseas would be exploring further areas of cooperation.

He said Iseas is already working with the Apsara Authority, which oversees the preservation of Angkor Wat, to hold a conference on Angkor next year.

The Royal Order of Sahametrei was established in 1948 by then King Norodom Sihanouk.

It is the second-highest honour in the Royal Orders of Cambodia, and is awarded to foreigners who have provided exceptional services to the country.

Keeping the past alive... for posterity

As head of a think-tank, Mr Krishnasamy Kesavapany is commissioning a series of biographies on Singapore's first-generation leaders. Why the big push to tell their stories now? What are the challenges? What does he hope to achieve?

BY ZAKIR HUSSAIN
POLITICAL CORRESPONDENT

For Iseas director Krishnasamy Kesavapany, one motivation behind the push to publish books on Singapore's first-generation leaders is that a younger generation of Singaporeans has grown up knowing little of these leaders. "These are stories which, if somebody does not take the trouble to record, will be forgotten," he says. ST PHOTO: JOYCE FANG

AMBASSADOR Krishnasamy Kesavapany was hooked on history as a nine-year-old boy in Kuala Lipis, Pahang.

His teacher, a Mr Halimi, would regale his Standard 3 (equivalent to Primary 3) pupils with stories from the Sejarah Melayu or Malay Annals, Indian epics and Chinese romances.

"He was a master storyteller who made history come alive," Mr Kesavapany, 73, recalls in an interview in his office at the Institute of Southeast Asian Studies (Iseas) on Heng Mui Keng Terrace in Pasir Panjang.

As his passion for history grew, the young Kesavapany studied in Liverpool for two years on a teaching scholarship.

When he returned, he was posted to teach in Penang, where he met his wife Padmini, a trainee teacher. They married in 1963 and have two sons.

Later, Mr Kesavapany, whose father was a rubber estate manager, pursued a history degree at the University of Malaya in Kuala Lumpur. After graduation, he worked in Singapore's then Labour Ministry for five years, before starting a 30-year career in the country's Foreign Service.

His varied diplomatic postings included London, Moscow and Geneva, where he was permanent representative to the United Nations. He is now non-resident Ambassador to Jordan.

Since his appointment as director of Iseas in 2002, Mr Kesavapany has not just rekindled his passion for the past.

He has taken on the daunting task of commissioning books on Singapore's first-generation leaders to tell the stories of these men and the choices they had to grapple with.

Referring to the period since self-government in 1959, he notes that "people see these five decades from various perspectives, and Iseas thought these different perspectives should be looked at".

This, he says, was why in the past two years, biographies of Singapore's first chief minister David Marshall and early Cabinet stalwarts S. Rajaratnam and Lim Kim San have been published.

They were written by law academic Kevin Tan, former Straits Times (ST) journalist and MP Irene Ng, and former ST journalist and Iseas fellow Asad Latif respectively.

In the pipeline are books on economic architect Goh Keng Swee and left-wing founding People's Action Party (PAP) member and Barisan Sosialis leader Lim Chin Siong.

Mr Kesavapany is hoping to get hold of the manuscript of Dr Lee Siew Choh's unpublished memoirs. Dr Lee, who died in 2002, led a group of dissident PAP legislative assemblymen to form Barisan Sosialis in 1961.

He is also thinking of a book on second chief minister Lim Yew Hock, as he feels that "the real story about him is still to be told".

Many Singaporeans believe Mr Lim sold off Christmas Island, which was part of Singapore, to Australia, but Mr Kesavapany says there is much more to it than that.

"These are facts which need to be put in the proper perspective. He was there at a very crucial time, when negotiations for self-government were under way," he says.

Also in the works are books on South-east Asian leaders, including one on the founders of Asean.

An Iseas bests eller, which has gone into its fifth reprint, is The Reluctant Politician by Dr Ooi Kee Beng – a biography of the late Malaysian home affairs minister and deputy prime minister Ismail Abdul Rahman.

Not rewriting history

ONE key motivation behind the biographical push for Mr Kesavapany is that more information is coming to the fore as time passes.

He notes that British colonial documents covering the 1950s and 1960s have since been declassified, giving scholars fresh insights into seminal events.

"It is not about rewriting history, but seeing whether there are other stories to be told," he says.

Another motivation is that a younger generation of Singaporeans has grown up knowing little of the first-generation leaders.

"Their main contributions, individually and collectively – if not recorded – will be forgotten in the mists of time. The younger generation will take them for granted.

"These are stories which, if somebody does not take the trouble to record, will be forgotten and, in another generation, will either become myths or distorted realities," he says.

Another driving force, he adds, is Mr Rajaratnam's vision that Iseas should be a place that publishes books which might not be otherwise produced, because they are not profitable. Mr Rajaratnam was a distinguished senior fellow at Iseas after he left politics.

He was a founding PAP member who went on to serve as Singapore's first Culture Minister and later Foreign Minister, before retiring from politics in 1988 as Senior Minister.

One draft currently being reviewed for publication is that of a book on the University of Malaya Socialist Club, a political debating society and student activist group in the 1950s and 1960s.

The club, whose prominent members included Ambassador-at-Large Tommy Koh, Iseas chairman Wang Gungwu and former leftist leaders Lim Hock Siew and S. Woodhull, played a role in the political struggle against the British, but later clashed with the PAP Government and was deregistered in 1971.

Mr Kesavapany makes it clear that all Iseas publications go through a stringent review process. Drafts of books are read by external reviewers "blindly" – they do not know the author, neither does the author know the identity of the reviewer.

"Comments are given and it is up to the writer to accept or not. But if the reviewers say this book is not fit enough to be published by Iseas, we take their word for it and tell the writer he can publish elsewhere. It's the only way to keep quality control," he says.

More access, please

ONE big challenge in writing history from a range of perspectives is the lack of access to confidential government records from self-governing Singapore's early years.

Doctoral candidate Seng Guo Quan had, in a letter to The Straits Times Forum page last month, asked for a more systematic declassification process for such documents.

In its reply, the Ministry of Information, Communications and the Arts said classified records would need to be downgraded before public release.

Some government agencies may have other reasons to withhold the records, such as security and privacy concerns, it added.

Asked for his views, Mr Kesavapany says that as a former civil servant he can see the need for certain documents to remain confidential.

"Revelations may embarrass persons still living, or interpretations will be made in a way that will not be in the interests of the state.

"For example, if you reveal something about a neighbouring country, even though the event occurred 40 years ago, there will still be rumblings. So it has to be measured up," he says.

But when he switches his hat to that of research institute head, he expresses the wish for a greater relaxation on access to past documents.

"Other people are already releasing them. You can go to archives in Britain, Australia, New Zealand," he notes,

Britain, as a former colonial master, kept volumes of records on developments in Singapore right up to and post-independence, as did Australia and New Zealand, which played a defence role in the region.

"So if we do not put out our version, people are going to write on the basis of what they can get from these other sources. Are we short-changing ourselves and our scholars?"

New issues emerge

ISEAS was established more than 40 years ago as an autonomous entity under the Ministry of Education, which means a large measure of academic freedom is invested in the institution.

"It has been the duty of the director, from its inception, to ensure this ethos of academic autonomy is maintained. It has led to certain uncomfortable positions, but by and large, it has been manageable," says Mr Kesavapany.

One area of autonomy is the books put out by Iseas, which have at times been critical, if objectively so, of countries or personalities in the region.

It is this fair-mindedness, he points out, that has built up Iseas' reputation as one of the leading think-tanks on South-east Asia.

Iseas was started principally to research and publish on countries in the region. As Asean expanded, its work has grown correspondingly.

A whole host of regional issues has emerged, from energy and security to migrant labour and climate change.

Two years ago, the Asean Studies Centre was set up within Iseas to research issues to do with Asean as an institution and as a process, and help the Asean Secretariat and member states.

More recently, the Nalanda-Sriwijaya Centre was set up to research ancient connections between and across India, China and South-east Asia.

The centre is named after Nalanda university in India, which thrived from the fifth to 12th centuries and is being revived by various parties, including Singapore, and after the powerful Sumatran kingdom – of which Singapore was a tiny part – that thrived from the seventh to 13th centuries.

Malaysia remains an abiding passion for Mr Kesavapany, a former Malaysian who was born in Kuala Lumpur, grew up in Pahang, taught in Penang, and served as Singapore's High Commissioner in Kuala Lumpur for five years from 1997.

Noting that "both countries are entering a mature relationship", he says he continues to keep a close watch on developments across the Causeway.

Telling old stories

IT BUGS Mr Kesavapany, however, that there seems to be a disconnect between Singapore's role as a port of call for traders in the region and the conspicuous absence of a maritime heritage museum to document those connections.

In a letter to the ST Forum page in February, he wrote that such a museum would add "immeasurably to the telling of the Singapore Story".

He is now helping to lay the groundwork for such a museum.

He notes that Sang Nila Utama, the 14th-century prince from Palembang who founded a city here and named it Singapura, came here by sea. So did Ming admiral Cheng Ho, and Sir Stamford Raffles who founded modern Singapore in 1819.

Then there are the findings of a Tang cargo vessel, which were displayed here five years ago, and now Oman's endowment of an Arab dhow, which is on its way to Singapore, he adds.

"A maritime museum can tell stories about the migrations of our forefathers, about trade, fights, and intermarriages."

He relates how, when he gave a talk at a top junior college recently, he was surprised to find out that students were mostly doing economics. No one mentioned history or geography.

"Unless you can instil a sense of curiosity and passion for knowing what happened before, all these efforts to bring out books on first-generation leaders will be in vain," he says.

One idea, he suggests, is for concerned parties to bring about lighter versions of some of these books, such as that on Mr Rajaratnam.

But he is adamant that a passion for the past, for what Singapore was, cannot simply be thrust upon youth.

"It's no use. It has to develop on its own," he says, adding that students need enough time at school to explore and develop a keenness in liberal arts subjects.

Still, he hopes the books coming out on the past will help others tell stories that fascinate and interest today's young, just as his teacher's stories lit up a spark in him many years ago.

zakirh@sph.com.sg

The Straits Times, 13 July 2004

TAN SUAN ANN

Iseas director K. Kesavapany (right) at the ceremony with Chilean ambassador Flisfisch.

Diplomat gets rare Chilean award

By **MAFOOT SIMON**

VETERAN diplomat K. Kesavapany is one of 100 people in the world to receive a rare, once-only honour.

The Chilean government has conferred on him the Presidential Medal of the Centennial of Pablo Neruda. Neruda is arguably the country's greatest poet of the last century.

The awards were given out yesterday in ceremonies held simultaneously in 65 countries to "distinguished public personalities from the cultural, academic and public arenas".

When asked why he had been given the award, the self-effacing director of the Institute of Southeast Asian Studies (Iseas) said: "Your guess is as good as mine."

Mr Kesavapany's ties with Chile go back a long way.

His first contact with the South American nation was in the 1970s when he was the Foreign Ministry's policy planning director dealing with Latin American countries.

It was then that he began to appreciate Chilean wine, he said at a quiet and dignified ceremony at the home of Chilean ambassador Angel Flisfisch, off Holland Road, yesterday.

Mr Kesavapany, 67, helped to set up the Chilean embassy here in 1979.

In the 1980s, he was involved in establishing the Pacific Economic Cooperation Council and Asia-Pacific Economic Cooperation and, in the 1990s, he worked closely with his Chilean counterparts at the World Trade Organisation.

His wife, Padmini, said: "Pany was very surprised. He said, 'I don't deserve to get this.' I think it's very nice of them to single him out for the award." Their two sons — both in their early 30s — also attended the ceremony.

Neruda, whose 100th birth anniversary is being celebrated with the awards, also had links with Singapore. The poet-diplomat was once an honorary consul to the country in 1931. He won the Nobel Prize in Literature in 1971, and died of leukaemia in 1973.

In his acceptance speech, Mr Kesavapany said that he had learnt of the award some 10 days ago. "Now after having heard what a great man Neruda was, I'm heavily burdened... I feel small."

Both Singapore and Chile are small countries, but "with big and noble visions", he said.

Chile is the Republic's 74th largest trading partner, with two-way trade totalling $155 million last year. Iseas is presently working with the Chile Foundation to develop a business model that, among other things, would create opportunities for businessmen in Southeast Asia and Latin America to interact and collaborate.

Diplomatic tango

MEMORIES. They are aplenty in the Kesavapany household. Photo albums, neatly labelled, line a massive shelf. Photographs of various hues adorn most of the walls and the family of four figures in most of them.

I did not get to meet all the family members but from the photographs I could trace the growth of MrK. Kesavapany's two sons Murali and Sashi – from boys all the way to young married men. The photographs also give you a glimpse into Mr Kesavapany's life as a diplomat in countries as varied as the UK, Russia and Jordan.

Then there is Benji, the border collie which lived a good 14 years and left the family heartbroken when it died. The pet was also responsible for the family moving into a landed property. Benji became part of the household while the Kesavapanys were in London but once the family moved to an apartment on their return to Singapore, the dog which was used to running around in the open compound in the London home could not take it. Seeing its agony, the family – especially Mr Kesavapany's wife Padmini – decided to move into a home with more space. Benji has long gone but the dog was instrumental in the family living in a home they have come to love.

Mr Kesavapany – his friends call him Pany – likes the quietness of the place tucked into the end of a side road in the Holland area. It is from here that he sets out on his morning walks, usually to the Ghim Moh market area, before he gets ready for his daily drive to the Institute of Southeast Asian Studies in Pasir Panjang where he is the director.

"I supervise the research work done at the institute. We also conduct public outreach programmes on a variety of topics. This involves networking with other institutes and organisations, both within and outside Singapore," says Mr Kesavapany, admitting he is lucky to be working full time at the age of 73.

That's not the only work that the man who was Singapore's high commissioner to Malaysia for five years from March 1997 is involved with.

Memories never fade... the walls of Mr Kesavapany's home are dotted with framed photographs.
PHOTO: ARUN RAMU

K. KESAVAPANY
Director, Institute of Southeast Asian Studies

Looking at me now, you would hardly believe that I dance the tango quite exquisitely!
– Mr Kesavapany

"I am also Singapore's non-resident ambassador to Jordan. This involves travelling to that country at least three times a year. I also serve on a number of boards including the Energy Studies Institute and the Hindu Endowments Board. My main NGO activity at the moment is to serve as the president of the Singapore Indian Association."

As president, Mr Kesavapany is using T20 cricket to draw in more Indian expats and new Indian Singaporeans to integrate with the local community.

Cricket, though, is not MrKesavapany's favourite sport. He prefers golf.

"Golf is my favoured form of relaxation. However, as it takes four hours per game, I don't get to play enough. I make up with hour-long walks. Both Padmini and I love watching Tamil and Malayalam TV shows. So the evenings are taken up, when we are not out for social engagements. Reading for work and pleasure is another activity I enjoy," says the diplomat.

Both Mr Kesavapany and his wife were born in Kuala Lumpur. His father was a Telugu from Vellore who worked as a manager in a rubber estate. When the young Pany finished his schooling in Ipoh, he was offered a teacher's training scholarship in Liverpool. He spent more than two years there and picked up ballroom dancing, something he says not many people know about. "Of course, looking at me now, you would hardly believe that I dance the tango quite exquisitely!" he says with a smile.

He was posted to Penang on his return and that's where he met trainee teacher Padmini, who is Malayalee. After they got married, he decided to join the university and read history in Kuala Lumpur. That paved the way for his job in Singapore.

By the time he graduated, Singapore and Malaysia had parted ways and he was offered a job by Singapore's Public Service Commission. He wanted to join the foreign service but ended up in the labour ministry. After five years his dream came true and he was posted to Singapore's embassy in Jakarta. Around this time, he also took up Singapore citizenship.

Even as he worked as a diplomat, Mr Kesavapany never lost sight of furthering his education. While in London, he took his master's degree from the School of Oriental and African Studies, specialising in south-east Asia and the Cambodian conflict.

His diplomatic skills were put to the test when he organised the first ministerial conference of the World Trade Organisaton (WTO) in Singapore in 1996. He considers this one of the highlights of his diplomatic career. Following his return from Geneva the same year, where he was ambassador to the UN and the WTO, he was made Singapore's high commissioner to Malaysia.

It was not the best of times. Malaysians had taken exception to Mr Lee Kuan Yew's comment on the crime situation in Johor but, being a savvy diplomat, Mr Kesavapany rode the storm and finished his term still wearing his smile.

No wonder he's still going strong in his 70s.

patrickj@sph.com.sg

CHAPTER 15

The Change that I Wish to See

After the decade at ISEAS, I was happy to move on and venture into new pastures and indulge in activities that I could not do so before. I had dreams of playing golf three times a week, reading all the books I had set aside to read, and to see matinee shows at the theatres. I came to know that Singapore senior citizens were given the special rate of $4 per film show, with coffee and popcorn thrown in! However, this was not meant to be.

Some of my friends thought I would go into mental decay if I did not keep myself busy. Through Mr Nathan, I was introduced to the Dean of Social Sciences at the Singapore Management University (SMU), Professor James Tang. He invited me to teach a course in International Relations of Southeast Asia. This thrilled me no end as I was happy to return to my first love, teaching. However, the experience at SMU came as a cultural shock.

The students were no longer the docile students from my previous time as a teacher. They questioned, argued and challenged their teacher. With online resources like Google at hand, they were up to the mark where information was concerned. The dressing and behaviour of the students I came across were somewhat disconcerting at first. Some of them even ate and drank in the classrooms. Gradually, I came to accept that this was a new norm of student behaviour. I enjoyed the course and I believe the students enjoyed it, too.

The late Mr Nathan, a Distinguished Fellow at the university, was outraged by the dressing and the demeanour of the students when he came to give a talk to my class at my invitation. Later, he berated me for tolerating this kind of behaviour on the part of the students. By now, I was accustomed to the ways of the students. I told him gently, "Mr Nathan, we adapt to their ways, or we lose them."

The following year, at the invitation of Dean Kishore Mahbubani, I joined the Lee Kuan Yew School of Public Policy as an Adjunct Professorial Fellow. I am still with the School and give lectures to visiting groups such as from Japan.

I also became involved in several social institutions. Through Ambassador Tommy Koh, I was introduced to the then Chairman, Euleen Goh, and director, Jean Tan, of the Singapore International Foundation (SIF), who offered me the appointment of Governor on the Board. This was a pleasurable experience as it reconnected me to my days in MFA when I was in charge of its Technical Assistance Programme. I represented SIF on various trips to Cambodia, Indonesia, Thailand, Malaysia and Sri Lanka. The programme that I am most keen to promote is "Water for Life", which brings clean water to isolated communities. The scope and value of public diplomacy that SIF is engaged in should be made better known to Singaporeans.

This is a task that Ambassador Ong Keng Yong, who took over from Euleen, is seriously engaged in.

I was also involved in the setting up of the Indian Heritage Centre (IHC), which was the brainchild of the late Dr S Balaji Sadasivan, the then Senior Minister of State for Foreign Affairs and Culture. Even though he was unwell at that point in time, he put in a lot of effort to make the IHC what it is today. Upon Dr Sadasivan's demise, Mr S Iswaran, the then Senior Minister of State for Trade & Industry and Education, took over the Chairmanship of the Steering Committee. At the working level, there were two committees involved in the setting up of the Centre. One of them was the Concept and Content Sub-committee headed by Ambassador Gopinath Pillai. I was his Deputy.

The other committee was the Design and Construction Sub-committee, which was headed by my good friend Ambassador R Jayachandran with Ashvinkumar Kantilal as his Deputy. Dr Gauri Krishnan headed the working group and played an important part in setting up the Centre in 2014. The Centre was opened officially by Prime Minister Lee Hsien Loong. Currently, S Saravanan is the Centre Manager and Nalina Gopal, the curator. Several notable exhibitions pertaining to Indians and Indian culture, including the latest exhibition that was launched on 6 September 2018, entitled *Chetti Melaka of the Straits: Rediscovering Peranakan Indian Communities,* have been organised.

Persuaded by Mr M Bala Subramanion, the first Asian Postmaster General of Singapore, I became a member of the Singapore Indian Association (SIA).

An organisation with a 94-year-old history, it needed to be revitalised. Building on the contributions of prominent lawyer Leslie Netto and his predecessors, Mr MV Rajendran (Eddie Raj) became the chairman of the new management committee. He was supported by Shabbir Hassanbhai, R Narayana Mohan, Gurucharan Singh, Kirpa Ram Vij, Suresh Kalpathy, V Giri Mudeliar, Maneesh Tripathi, P Thirunalkerasu, Jayaprekash Jagateesan, Dinesh Singh, VP Jothi, Haider Sittiwala, M Rajaram and Dr Kamal Bose. My son, Murali, became the Chairman of the Board of Games. Later, S Devendran took over from Murali. Two years later, I took over the presidency of the SIA.

In 2007, the new committee took the bold step of obtaining an $800,000 loan from the Indian Overseas Bank to renovate the premises. The committee members stood as guarantors for the loan. Hearing about this loan, a noted philanthropist, Mr SM Jaleel, stepped in and paid off the loan. The SIA will always be indebted to Mr Jaleel for his generosity. Well-known for his philanthropy, Mr Jaleel has set up a Foundation to serve the community at large and the Indian community in particular. I am proud to be a Director of this Foundation.

In the last seven years, the Association has largely succeeded in its goal of being involved in the areas of intra-community and inter-community integration through sports. With the help of companies like Olam and the State Bank of India, the SIA organised the Olam Cup and held the National Day Sixes Sports Carnival, featuring cricket, football and hockey tournaments.

A new phase of the organisation's activities was to focus on reshaping the Welfare Fund. Originally, the Welfare Fund was set up to look into the repatriation of stranded Indian indentured labour. With the High Commission of India taking over this activity, there was no longer the need for the Singapore Indian Association to deal with this issue. The Welfare fund was, therefore, reformatted to help students in need of bursaries and scholarships. However, with the Singapore Indian Development Association (SINDA) and the Singapore Indian Education Trust (SIET) as well as Hindu temples and other organisations playing this role, the Committee decided to establish a programme called "Helping People from Falling through the Cracks". As this is one of my core social service interests, I spend a considerable amount of time developing this programme. This Committee consists of Leslie Netto, M Bala Subramanion, Professor Kamal Bose, Ameerali and myself, with Sivarajah acting as Secretary.

The Association commissioned the publication of two books, one by Nilanjana Sengupta entitled *Singapore, My Country,*[39] which was about M Bala Subramanion. Mr Bala turns 93 this year and continues to be an active member of the SIA. The second book was *The Life and Times of a Social Worker* by KV Veloo.[40] Both books were well-received by the public. If not for the publication of these two books issued under the auspices of the Singapore Indian Association, the valuable

[39] Nilanjana Sengupta, *Singapore, My Country: Biography of M Bala Subramanion* (World Scientific Publishing, 2016).

[40] KV Veloo, *Life and Times of a Social Worker: A Personal Memoir* (Wee Kim Wee Centre, SMU, 2014).

contributions by these two men to the community and society would have disappeared into the mist of history. After six years, I was happy to hand over the presidency of the Singapore Indian Association to an old friend, VV Giri. With an enthusiastic team, I am confident that he will lead the Association to greater heights.

Concomitant with my social and welfare activities, I accepted the appointment of a Term Trustee in SINDA. Headed by DPM Tharman Shanmugaratnam as Chairman and Minister Indranee Rajah as President, SINDA is well known for its pioneering work in raising the educational level of its community. SINDA is also addressing the social and welfare needs of the community.

I was also appointed to the Board of Advisors of the Hindu Endowments Board led by Ambassador Jayachandran. Mr Rajan Krishnan is the Chairman of the Hindu Advisory Board. Both boards work closely in ensuring that the needs of the Hindu community are well-served. They have become agents for change in Singapore. This is particularly seen in the way the holy festival of Thaipusam has been managed in recent years.

I also serve as an adviser to Singapore Indian Educational Trust (SIET). Over the past 51 years, SIET has extended close to $9 million in bursaries and loans to more than seven thousand deserving students who were in need of financial assistance to pursue their education.

As a former Advisor to the Singapore Indian Chamber of Commerce and Industry (SICCI), I am delighted that the new team led by Dr T

Chandroo has been energised. Initiatives aimed at exploring business opportunities in the burgeoning Chinese market are noteworthy developments.

One of the self-help organisations that I admire greatly is the Muslim Kidney Action Committee (MKAC). It was set up principally to change the mindset of Muslims towards the issue of organ donation. The MKAC has expanded its scope to lend support to kidney patients and their families. My good friend, Ameerali, is the CEO of this organisation. An expert in the field of safety in the workplace, he is a Justice of the Peace (JP) and recipient of many awards. He is highly skilled in motivating the youth to pay forward to the community at large. I am a staunch supporter of MKAC's activities.

Whenever people ask me: "So Pany, have you retired?" I say, "No, I have merely moved on."

In the middle of 2013, I found myself running three social programmes. One of them was initiated by DPM Tharman Shanmugaratnam, for the aftercare of Indian drug addicts. It was found that a high proportion of addicts at Changi prison were Indians. Also, there was an increasing rate of recidivism. The Indian Community Aftercare Council (ICAC) was therefore established under the auspices of SINDA, to come to grips with this problem. Basically, the mandate was to galvanise the community, impress upon them the seriousness of the problem, and recruit volunteers who would be trained as befrienders by the Singapore Prison Services (SPS). These befrienders would help discharged prisoners reintegrate into society.

There is a general impression that Indians are not inclined towards volunteerism. This turned out to be not the case. Within five months of the establishment of ICAC, about 60 volunteers were recruited and 30 were sent to SPS for training as befrienders. The Council was launched on 17 January 2015 by Mr Iswaran, Minister in the Prime Minister's Office and the Second Minister for Home Affairs and Trade and Industry. Among the members of the council were Mr KV Veloo, a retired social service officer, Mr Ameer Ali and Mr Saravanan.

Many of the initiatives are meant to provide greater support to those in need in our society. For instance, most of the cases that "Helping People from Falling through the Cracks" dealt with were people living on $500 or below a month. One such case was a severely diabetic 45-year-old man who was living in a one-room Housing and Development Board flat. He was brought to my attention by my former colleague, Ambassador Simon D'Cruz, who volunteers with "Willing Hearts". His poor health meant that he could not work. He was given $350 from the Central Singapore Community Development Centre (CDC). Most of it went towards paying for his utilities, with little left for anything else. His main meal of the day came from an organisation called Willing Hearts. The fund provided him with $400 dollars more per month, for a period of six months.

Another case was a 32-year-old man, who had gone in and out of prison four times. After rehabilitation, he got married. Soon enough, his wife was with child. Unfortunately, his child was born premature and needed special formula milk, which cost $78 per week. The man also became afflicted with a flesh-eating disease, which meant that he could not go to work. His wife, too, could not go to work, as she had to stay at home to look after their newborn child. The family of three lived on $400 per month from the CDC. The fund gave him $400 more per month, to cover the cost of the newborn child's milk needs. There are so many cases like this, where people in bad situations find themselves mired in more problems, making breaking out of the poverty cycle nearly impossible.

These experiences, gained from working on the ground, led me to ponder over the issue of growing income inequality in Singapore. To their credit, the government and civil society are seized with this problem. I feel, however, that there should be a fundamental change in the approach taken to mitigate the problems that the underclass faces.

We have families in Singapore struggling to cover their basic living expenses. There is a need for a new way to look after the underclass. In any case, in a wealthy country such as ours, why must the poor continue to scrape the bottom of the barrel? Are they not entitled to a modicum of dignity, by having a basic standard of living?

There must be a baseline, a minimum standard of living for those earning less than $3,000. From the baseline, people will be able to progress and improve their lives on their own. If we do not even have a baseline, then you will have growing groups of people who are never going to catch up with the rest of society. The poor will fall back further, even as the rest of Singapore progresses. This is already happening. Recently, I spoke to a social worker. She told me that it is getting increasingly difficult to do her job, as there are simply too many cases to handle, and asked if she could refer some of the cases to SINDA or to the Singapore Indian Association.

Several years ago, I was inspired by an article in *The Straits Times* by correspondent Aaron Low, who suggested setting up a basic pension for the aged poor in Singapore. He argued that there was a need to help the elderly who did not have enough in their CPF accounts for retirement. The CPF scheme is based on compulsory savings deducted from a worker's own monthly wage. Hence, only those who work would have CPF.

In his incisive article, Aaron Low, discussed the plight of families with "zero savings" who got by "using their meager wages to support their own families and their aged parents. They save by eating meat only once a week, or using candles to save on electricity."[41]

The usual suggestion put forward for those with little or no CPF balance was to prepare for retirement by monetising the value of their flat by renting out a room or by downsizing. However, this suggestion still leaves those without their own HDB flats and little family support hanging. These people have fallen through the cracks and have to constantly worry about covering their living expenses. Setting up a pension fund will address the worries of the elderly poor and give them greater peace of mind in their twilight years.

[41] Aaron Low, "Pension to give peace of mind to the elderly poor" (*The Straits Times*, 3 January 2015) <http://www.asiaone.com/singapore/pension-give-peace-mind-elderly-poor>

Piggybacking on the idea of a pension, I am going to stick my neck out here and ask why have it just for the aged poor. Why not have it for anyone whose per capita household income is below a certain quantum? The Public Assistance Scheme is meant for citizens and permanent residents, and eligibility criteria include not being able to work due to old age, illness or disability, and having little or no means of income and little or no family support.

From my own experience, the amount provided is not enough, and there exists a large band of households just above those who are benefiting from the scheme, and they, too, are struggling to cover daily living expenses. While there are targeted efforts to help this group offset living costs through the provision of food vouchers, transport and medical subsidies, they are not enough of a leg up. Further, these concessions are arbitrary; they come and go. The underclass needs a source of sustainable income that is free to be used to meet their individual needs.

Let me give you an example to illustrate this point. The diabetic man to whom I referred earlier in this chapter is unable to take public transport to the hospital for treatment, as going up and down the bus poses difficulties. He has to take a taxi to the hospital, and each trip costs him $20. He makes about four trips to the hospital each month. Transport alone eats up half of the $350 given to him by the CDC. These are micro problems that grant providers will rarely come to know about and take into account.

I had personally gone out to meet this man with my friend, Ambassador Simon D' Cruz. When I met him, he was very despondent. He was born a Hindu, and then changed his religion to Christianity, thinking the change might do something for him. So you have Hindu Gods on the left side of the cabinet shelf in the living room, and the Christian cross on the other side. Nearing the end of the visit, he said that he felt like two angels had come to see him, and that he was touched by the fact that people out there cared for him. The human touch and quality of someone reaching out is vital to the administration of social welfare.

Lastly, I am going to tell you a story of this 16-year-old girl who was referred to the Singapore Indian Association. Her father had come from India, married a local, who, after childbirth, passed away. Her father returned to India and started his own family there, while she was left in Singapore, under the charge of her maternal grandparents. Her grandparents had not registered her birth, and so she did not have citizenship. The family faced difficulties when it came to Junior College, where she had to pay up to $1,000 per term in fees. When I heard of her case, I felt that she needed help. She was a human being in a bad situation, through absolutely no fault of her own. The Singapore Indian Association eventually paid off her debt of $4,200. One good Samaritan heard of her plight, and paid for the rest of her education fees, which came up to $17,000.

Maybe I will have people coming to tell me that I am too utopian, for wanting the social system to be able to provide those earning less than

$3,000 with a minimum standard of living. What is certain, though, is that the question of falling through the cracks is real and present. It is necessary to take a systematic approach in addressing the problems of the underclass.

Page 14 February 24, 2017 **tabla!** **SINGAPORE**

IA going strong at 94

FROM PAGE 13

In recent challenging times, Mr Subramanion, who was president from 1964 to 1968, felt the need to nudge Mr Kesavapany.

"I had known him for a long time, even before he joined the diplomatic service. I knew his capabilities, his experience in international affairs, his charisma and ability to get things done and lead the association. I thought he would be the most suitable person to lead, (with) this daunting task of enhancing IA's ambiance," he said.

In sharing the troubles faced, Mr Kesavapany felt the need for intervention, as the club's fortunes were not what they were.

"If we didn't do something, the place might even disappear. We built on what past leaders did — rebuilt, refocused and this even caught the attention of the Indian Government," he said.

Mr Jothi said: "It was slow and challenging but we have made tremendous progress especially over the last five years.

"We are justified in claiming that we have succeeded in terms of restoring the prestige and uplifting all aspects of the association, in the social, cultural and sports arenas. Of course, it is not an end game – more needs to be done."

Special visitor... The late A.P.J. Abdul Kalam (left) visiting IA in 2008. With him are Mr Netto (extreme right), Mr Kesavapany (centre) and Mr Jothi (third from right) (Below) Mr Kesavapany receiving the Pravasi Bharatiya Samman Award from India's President Pranab Mukherjee. PHOTOS: IA

Forging Ahead Towards a Common Destiny

Putting things in historical context, Mr Netto summarised: "As Passage of Indians reveals, IA was indeed relevant during British times because, by and large, the British left the communities to care for themselves. The British were willing to help when requests were made by well organised groups in the communities. With independence, this was no more the case.

"The government introduced Sinda and there are community centres that care for Indian welfare, including sports. We have lost much of our relevance. But it is good for our community to have a place of our own. We should emphasise sports with a view to keeping our youth away from mischief. IA is ideal because of its history. It would do Singapore proud."

Elaborating on its current direction, Mr Kesavapany said: "We are now plugged into inter-community activities which the Government promotes to bring about racial cohesiveness. In addition, we recently renovated the clubhouse but have kept fees as low as possible to make it accessible for everyone to join the association.

"We also work very closely with the Indian High Commission — whenever there are visiting delegations, these are opportunities to interact and build relationships. Finally, our cricketing prowess as an SCA League winner is attracting members of the younger generation. The future of the club needs a new and younger set of leaders to take over and chart the future of the association."

Mr Subramanion said: "We have a place in Singapore, as Singaporeans or Indian residents, within a multi-racial society. That is why IA is an important place. Now is the time for all Indians in Singapore to support the Indian Association by becoming a member."

The Pravasi Bharatiya Samman Award is an accolade not just for its past glory but also for IA's current achievements and vision, to foster a stronger sense of community for all Indians for greater contributions within our multiracial society towards a common destiny.

➡ tabla@sph.com.sg

CHAPTER 16

The Rotary Movement: Service above Self

My entry into the Rotary world came via the Rotary Club of KL di Raja. It is the custom of the club to invite serving Heads of Mission to become Honorary Members. At the invitation of then President Dato Kulasegaran, I became a member and entered the fascinating world of Rotary. I made many good friends like Tan Sri L Krishnan, Dato Hanif and Frank Lim among others.

During troubled times when bilateral relations were rocky, these Rotarian friends stood by me. I also helped to form a symbiotic relationship between the Rotary Club of KL di Raja and the Rotary Club of Raffles City (RCRC). This relationship has stood the test of time.

Returning to Singapore, after my Kuala Lumpur posting, I joined the RCRC. I came to know the Rotary movement which has done, and continues to do, a lot of good work worldwide. Unfortunately, it is viewed by some as a "rich man's club", with the members only dining and socialising. When ESM Goh Chok Tong asked me, "What does Rotary do?" I felt I had to set the record straight. Fellow member, Namratha Lakshmi, and I produced a booklet in 2018 called *Rotary – Service above Self*. Among other things, the booklet tells the story of how Rotary has been instrumental in the eradication of polio. For the next three years, it has committed itself to raising $150 million, which will be matched 1–2 by the Bill & Melinda Gates Foundation, yielding $450 million for polio eradication activities, including immunisation and surveillance.

Among the other projects that the Rotary Movement is involved with are providing clean water, addressing the issues of domestic violence and health related problems. Prevention of blindness is a major component of Rotary's social welfare work. With its members spread worldwide, the Rotary Movement is able to respond to the call "Think Global, Act Local". My own club, RCRC, has "two Crown Jewels" to its credit: the Dyslexia Association of Singapore (DAS) and the Crohns & Colitis Society (CCS). The first is a project aimed at bringing awareness about dyslexia to Singaporeans. On the suggestion of then RCRC president George Abraham, the club's chairman of Community Services Dr Jimmy Daruwalla, headed a working group to see what could be done about this condition that was rarely talked about.

My introduction to this group came as a result of an invitation to my wife, Padmini, a teacher trained in the UK in Special Needs education. I went along as her driver and ended up by being co-opted into the group which later became DAS.

Over the next 25 years, as current President of DAS, Mr Eric Lee, has put it:[42]

[42] William Wan, *Clearly Different – Dyscovering the Differences* (Dyslexia Association of Singapore, 2017) p vi.

> We have spent the last 25 years attempting to unravel the world of differences that dyslexics face. From a small community service project led by our Founding President, the late Dr Jimmy Daruwalla in 1989, DAS has made great advances to become a significant charitable organization, with 13 learning centers across Singapore. It serves more than 3,500 students from preschools, primary and secondary schools, supported by a highly qualified, trained and dedicated group of 240 professionals and support staff for the thousands of students who have passed through our doors and graduated as confident individuals. We know that they will in turn become inspiring role models to others.

Dr Jimmy Daruwalla's wife, Roshen, was with him all through this journey. A Reading Centre has been named after her at DAS headquarters in Rex House.

My own small contribution to this saga was to secure DAS's first training centre in Kallang. My friend and MFA colleague, Mr Lee Chiong Giam, who was then Director of People's Association, put a Nissan Hut at our disposal. The debt that the Association owes to Chiong Giam for this gesture will never be forgotten.

Minister Mentor Lee Kuan Yew was also helpful by declaring that he was mildly dyslexic. This enabled many parents to drop their inhibitions about revealing that their children were dyslexic.

In a fitting tribute to Jimmy, DAS Patron, Mrs Goh Chok Tong, wrote the following words:[43]

> One man who has played an imitable role was the late Dr Jimmy Daruwalla. His passion and mission had not only founded DAS but lifted the organization to one great height after another. I believe that DAS will carry this baton and race forward with similar resolve and fervor.

The stellar roles played by the current Chief Executive Officer of DAS, Mr Lee Siang, his predecessor, Robin Moseley, and the staff of DAS deserve to be enshrined in the annals of DAS history. The full story of DAS can be found in a book written by my friend and kindred soul, Dr William Wan, entitled *Clearly Different – Dyscovering the Differences*.[44]

RCRC's other "crown jewel" is the establishment of the Crohns & Colitis Society (CCS). Started by my predecessor, Nidhi Swarup, it is a self-help group for those afflicted with this condition, as well as irritable bowel syndrome (IBS) patients. No such organisation existed to help IBS patients either, until 2011. In 2012, I took over as the President of the Rotary Club and continued to support Nidhi in her pioneering work. She also reached out to the Duke-NUS Medical School to promote research and training in this area. In Nidhi's own words:[45]

---

[43] William Wan, *Clearly Different – Dyscovering the Differences* (Dyslexia Association of Singapore, 2017) p iv.

[44] William Wan, *Clearly Different – Dyscovering the Differences* (Dyslexia Association of Singapore, 2017).

[45] Namratha Lakshmi & K Kesavapany, *Rotary – Service above Self* (Rotary Club of Raffles City, 2018) p 15.

> Had I not been a Rotarian, IBS patients would have been silently struggling with their own battles. I have met numerous patients who were diagnosed with Crohn's disease or Ulcerative colitis, 15, 20, 30 and 40 years old and had no idea that there were other IBS patients in Singapore!

The Society also has plans to expand its work to other countries in ASEAN.

It is customary or expected of the incoming Rotary Club president to initiate a social project during his tenure. While casting about for one, my long-time friend and fellow Rotarian, George Abraham, brought to my attention the existence of the Najeeven Centre, which runs a school for children of Mumbai sex workers. Established by the Mar Thomas Church in India, the Centre is working towards purchasing a transport vehicle to take the children to the nearest town, Kalyan, for official matters and treatment of major aliments, constructing three ponds for rain-water collection to address water scarcity in the village and providing uninterrupted power supply by the construction of solar panels on the roofs of the cottages in the village.

As all three segments of the project were in keeping with Rotary's social objectives, Rotary members, led by incumbent president, Mr Brian Tan, gave their full support and approved funding from the Club's resources. The Club will continue to monitor the progress of the project and ensure further assistance to this meaningful project.

In keeping with Rotary's ethos, it does not matter where the need is: what matters is stretching out a hand of assistance to those in need.

Champ for all

tabla!'s sixth Community Champion is a friend to many

PATRICK JONAS

He is one of the most recognisable faces at Indian gatherings. And that tells something about the man. Mr K. Kesavapany spent several decades in the diplomatic service, which meant he was overseas for long stretches.

Yet, he always kept in touch with the community here. When he retired and moved back to Singapore, he plunged deep into community affairs.

Next year Mr Kesavapany will turn 80 but he shows no signs of slowing down. He is connected with several organisations that work for the betterment of people. He is the president of the Singapore Indian Association, a Governor with the Singapore International Federation, a term trustee of Sinda, a member of the Hindu Advisory Board, an active member of the Dyslexia Association of Singapore and an adviser to Apsaras Arts.

Numerous others seek his wisdom and guidance. And Mr Kesavapany is generous with what he has to share.

The Indian Association (IA) is an organization with a long history, having been founded in 1925. It has a glorious past, with visitors like Nobel literature prize winner Rabindranath Tagore and India's first prime minister, Jawaharlal Nehru, who visited it thrice and laid the foundation stone of its building.

But as years went by, the club lost its focus and direction. There were taxes and debts to be paid and the building was run down. It had also acquired the reputation of being a drunkard's club.

However, there were some die-hard supporters of the association, especially Mr M. Bala Subramanion, who never gave up hope, and they convinced Mr Kesavapany to step in. He did, and along with then IA president Eddie Raj, turned the association around.

"We renovated the club and slowly got the community back. Because of the vacuum created by IA, Sinda had to be created. IA used to look after the interests of Indians here till then," said Mr Kesavapany.

IA has a welfare fund, which was set up more than 50 years ago with the aim of repatriating Indian indentured labour.

Now that such a need doesn't exist, Mr Kesavapany and his team converted it into a fund to provide bursaries for needy students.

But there were other Indian organisations doing that.

"So we felt we should go to the aid of people who are in danger of falling through the cracks. We created a programme called 'Helping people from falling through the cracks'. We collect our own money so we are able to respond faster. Recently we had a fund raising lunch. We raised $100,000 for this purpose," said Mr Kesavapany.

The fund has since helped several people. One was a 13-year-old girl who had a clenched fist. When the girl got to secondary school she was bullied because of that and she started cutting herself. She came from a poor family. Her father suffered from depression and a brother was autistic.

"We sent her to Karaikudi in Tamil Nadu where a doctor operated on her for free. Now four of her fingers have been straightened and the last one is being worked on," said Mr Kesavapany.

He has also used IA to reach out to Indians who are new citizens or PRs, through cricket. But he could not achieve the kind of success he wanted.

"Cricket, we thought, would be a medium to integrate but the experience has not been that good. New Indians use our grounds, play and leave. Some never even step into the club. They even bring their own food. So we are now working on football for the locals and working with Sinda," he said.

At Sinda, Mr Kesavapany is involved in social work. He is part of the Indian Community After Care Council, run by Sinda and the Hindu Endowments Board.

His efforts with cricket may not have brought the desired results but that has not stopped him from working to help new Indians integrate.

"We try and collaborate where we can. There has to be a consciousness on both sides," he added.

One of those who worked with him in his integration efforts is writer and artist Subina Khaneja, a former president of the Indian Women's Association.

Said Ms Khaneja: "His initiative to bring the community closer through the game of cricket was what brought me in touch with him, and gave me a chance to work along with him and experience his magnanimity, his graciousness in dealing with each and every person. As president of the Indian Women's Association he was my support, especially in our Integration efforts. Above all, it is his espirit lumiere, the light of his spirit, that makes him a true champion of the community."

Mr Kesavapany is quite happy with the progress made by IA and said it is time for him to step down.

His deputy at IA, Mr V.P. Jothi said Mr Kesavapany's leadership has brought about a profound change and provided new impetus to the 90 year old organisation.

He said Mr Kesavapany completely immersed himself in community work after he retired from public service and this is something which makes him stand out from his peers.

"He applied his innate leadership qualities and his public stature with humility to connect and contribute to diverse Indian community interest groups in the arts, cultural, education, social and charity space," said Mr Jothi, who added that he and his fellow members at IA are "happy and proud that Mr Kesavapany is receiving this prestigious tabla! Community Champion Award".

Mr Kesavapany has also used the skills he learnt in publishing books at the Institute of South-east Asian Studies, where he was

Memorable moments... Mr Kesavapany being presented with a cheque of $10,000 by State Bank of India's Country Head Soma Sankara Prasad (third from right), (others from left) Mr Patrick Jonas, Mr Chandra Das, Ms Sim Ann, Mr Warren Fernandez and Tamil Murasu editor J. Rajendran.Mr Kesavapany is giving $5,000 each to the Dyslexia Association of Singapore and the Indian Association Welfare Fund.

For a good cause... (Left) At the book launch of Mr K.V. Veloo with late Mr S R Nathan in 2014. (Below left) Being awarded the Ekta Integration Award by IWA in 2013. (Below) at the panel discussion last year titled "Meeting the reintegration challenges of Indian ex-offenders into society" at the inaugural Indian Community Aftercare Forum.
PHOTOS: FILE, TIMOTHY DAVID

tabla! COMMUNITY CHAMPION 2016 SUPPORTED BY SBI STATE BANK OF INDIA

director, to good use for the community. He has married publishing of books with rasing funds for a cause.

"At the Institute, I learnt to be an educational entrepreneur where you can use entrepreneurial skills for educational purposes and when I came to IA, I found I could use it for social work. So I published a book by social worker K.V. Veloo and gave him $10k for writing it. He returned the amount to the IA welfare fund."

He recently facilitated the publishing of a book on independent Singapore's first post-master general Bala Subramanion, who donated part of the proceeds to IA's Welfare Fund.

"Currently, we have sold more than a 1,000 copies of the book. The third book is in the works. It is on Mr J.Y. Pillay. There are many other stories to be told," said Mr Kesavapany.

Another organisation that is close to Mr Kesavapany's heart is the Dyslexia Association of Singapore (DAS). In the eighties, the Rotary Club of Raffles City asked one of its members, the late Dr Jimmy Daruwalla who was tabla!'s first Community Champion, to set up an association to help dyslexic students. At that time Mr Kesavapany's wife Padmini was a teacher of special needs children at Dover Court Preparatory School and she was invited by the Rotary Club for her views.

"I went as my wife's chauffeur and ended up as a committee member," said Mr Kesavapany, a member of the DAS exco. He said the initial years of DAS were difficult as many Singaporeans did not want to admit their children were dyslexic. He feels that neither DAS, nor Dr Daruwalla — who was president of the association for 25 years — has been sufficiently recognized for its work.

Mr Kesavapany worked closely with Dr Daruwalla, who died in July, to promote the work of DAS.

That was not the only loss this year for tabla!'s new Community Champion.

Mr Kesavpany was very close to the late Singapore president S R Nathan and their friendship goes a long way back. Mr Kesavapany attributes his links to so many people in the Indian community to Mr Nathan.

"Once you get to know Mr Nathan you get to know a lot of people and you become part of the community," said Mr Kesavapany.

He says he is a firm believer in karma. Most days he leaves the house in the morning and tries to have lunch outside. This ensures he is able to meet people.

He also feels that any organisation or post is what you want to make of it. "You can either do the minimum or you can do much more," he said.

He recited Omar Khayaam's lines from the Rubiyat when asked for the secret of his calmness.

The Moving Finger writes; and, having writ,
Moves on: nor all thy Piety nor
Wit Shall lure it back to cancel half a Line,
Nor all thy Tears wash out a Word of it.

"That's my approach to life. Just take it as it comes. Sometimes good, sometimes bad. Sometimes sad, sometimes happy. So I am not a man stressed with anything," he said.

patrickj@sph.com.sg

CHAPTER 17

My Inter-Faith Journey

Before going into the story of how a "non-religious" person became involved in this 71-year-old organisation, let me say a few words about the Inter-Religious Organisation (IRO). Started in 1947 by a group of eminent civic and religious personalities, including Maulana Siddique, Malcom Macdonald and Dato Onn Bin Jaffar, the organisation has stood the test of time. Its main achievement has been the socialisation of religion, through regular interactions between and among the members of the ten religious organisations represented in the IRO Council. Through such interactions, the Council has helped to entrench one of the founding principles of our Nation-state, which is "Maintenance of Religious Harmony". Together with its twin pillar of racial integration, Singapore has been able to be an oasis of peace and stability since its independence over the past 50 years.

September 11, 2001, the rise of racial and religious extremism, and the advent of social media have brought fresh challenges to both the government and civil society practitioners, including the IRO.

In June 2016, by virtue of the rotation method practised at the IRO, it became the turn of the Hindu Endowments and Hindu Advisory

Boards to nominate one of their members for the post of President of the IRO Council. My friends, Ambassador R Jayachandran and Mr Rajan Krishnan, put forward my name for the post. At the age of 79, and with no experience in the management of religious matters, both intra and inter, I was reluctant to take on the job. One of the hardest things I found was to say "no" to both these fine friends.

However, intervention came in the form of the late Mr Nathan, who was then the IRO's Patron. Ever mindful of my interest, Mr Nathan felt that I should wait a year before taking on the post of president of the organisation as this would give me time to familiarise myself with its workings. He persuaded Mr Rustom Ghadiali, a veteran and two-time president, to take on the post.

This gave me one year to familiarise myself with the running of the IRO Council and getting to know the 30 members. Swami Vimokshananda and Shriniwas Rai were the other members representing the Hindu Faith. Before I knew it, I was in the hot seat and assumed the presidency of the IRO in March 2017.

At its first meeting, the Council adopted the "Three Rs Initiative": Relevance, Reach and Rehabilitation.

- "Relevance" – To examine the raison d'être for the founding of IRO in 1947 and see what adjustments need to be made to meet the current geopolitical and religious scenario.
- "Reach" – To spread the message of inter-religious harmony beyond existing boundaries and via social media.

- "Rehabilitation" – To be on the lookout for signs and signals of religious extremism in the population, especially youth.

The IRO's relevance was noticeable in the increase in the number of visitors to its office in the Ministry of National Development (MND) Annex Building in Maxwell Road. After visiting the Harmony Centre in the same building, visitors made it a point to visit the IRO office and meet its members.

At meetings outside the office, the IRO also made its presence felt. For example, during the visit of Prince Charles, the Prince of Wales, to the Harmony Gallery in the Masjid An-Nahdhah, he said there was no organisation like the IRO in the United Kingdom and he was taking back the ideas he had gathered on the maintenance of religious harmony in Singapore.

Another notable visitor was Indonesian Minister of Religious Affairs, Bapak Lukman Hakim Saifuddin, in 2017. Arranged by Imam Habib Hassan of the Masjid Ba'alwi, the minister noted the similarity of views held by Indonesia and Singapore on the subject of religious harmony. The minister's call for an increase in interactions between the peoples of both countries was welcomed warmly by the Singapore side.

A third important visitor was a former minister from the United Arab Emirates. While on a private visit to Singapore, he had heard about the IRO and its work. During the exchange of views, he suggested bilateral collaboration in this area. Apart from these official exchanges, an increasing number of Singaporeans, including schoolchildren and foreigners, visited the Harmony Gallery and the IRO office. These visits have proved useful in advancing the relevance of religious harmony as a tool for nation-building.

The latest was during Indian Prime Minister Narendra Modi's visit to Singapore on 31 May 2018. The event was the immersion of Mahatma Gandhi's ashes at Clifford Pier. The High Commissioner of India to Singapore, Mr Jawed Ashraf, arranged especially for IRO representatives to be present at the event.

The second objective of IRO is "Reach". The IRO Council felt that it was not enough to interlocute with and among the "converted", that is, people in the city centre. It was important to take the message of religious harmony into the heartlands and get religious institutions there involved. The first of these "To The Heartland" initiatives was held in Yishun with the enthusiastic endorsement from Senior Parliamentary Secretary Associate Professor Dr Muhammad Faishal Ibrahim, at a meeting held in the Sree Narayana Mission in 2017. Invitations extended to Masjid Darul Makmur, a Taoist group and the Sree Maha Mariamman Temple met with an enthusiastic response. Officials from the Ministry of Culture, Community & Youth (MCCY) and the Inter-Racial and Religious Confidence Circles (IRCC) provided logistical support. The dialogue that followed, chaired by Dr William Wan, saw an open exchange of views.

The third objective is "Rehabilitation". In the light of the spread of extremism, particularly via social media, it is apparent that more eyes and ears are needed to address this growing social menace. As women, by virtue of their homemaking roles, are the primary defenders of faith, the IRO has strengthened the Women of Faith Wing led by Sister Maria. The numbers have increased and activities have been added to promote inter-religious harmony among women.

Special mention must be made of the Prayer Group headed by octogenarian Harban Singh. The group is called upon for prayers at both public events, such as the passing out parade of National Service Officer Cadets and private functions like the opening of companies. The activities of the Prayer Group have served to increase the profile of the IRO.

On 30 November 2018, ESM Goh Chok Tong graciously accepted IRO's invitation for him to be the second patron of the IRO, following the late Mr Nathan. This would give the organisation a tremendous boost and profile its standing both within and beyond Singapore.

There is still a lot of work to be done. The goal should be to have an ASEAN-wide network of IROs. I am confident that my successor, Mr Ben J Benjamin, and his Council Members will do this and achieve much more.

CHAPTER 18

My Encounter with APJ Abdul Kalam

On 21 July 2018, 500 people came together in P Govindasamy Pillai (PGP) Hall to mark the second anniversary of the demise of the late President of India, Abdul Kalam. The occasion was also to launch the Abdul Kalam Vision Society (AKVS), which would honour and remember this great statesman of India, popularly known as the People's President.

Speaking on the occasion, Indian High Commissioner Jawad Ashraf highlighted some noteworthy achievements of the late President. Having worked with Dr Kalam, he was able to give personal examples of how the scientist-turned-statesman had made a difference to the lives of the people. He added that the ideas and scientific temper that Abdul Kalam espoused were not limited to national boundaries but had international relevance.

Commending the Indian community in Singapore for the effort to set up AKVS, Mr Jawad Ashraf suggested that some knowledge-based events should be held.

The next speaker, Dr VK Ponraj, Scientific Adviser to the late president, commented that the late Dr Kalam always looked to the future. Describing him as a "borderless scientist", Dr Ponraj said, "He (Dr Kalam) gave sustainable solutions to many of the world's problems in areas such as healthcare, environment, agriculture, energy, water and infrastructure." Dr Ponraj, too, hoped that the AKVS would play a vital part in making the vision of the late president a reality.

Speaking in my capacity as president of the AKVS, I said there were five major points in the late Dr Kalam's life and legacy which were of relevance to Singapore. These were religious harmony, meritocracy, addressing income inequality, science for the benefit of society, and inspiring youth to look towards the future.

I added, "Dr Kalam's inspirational life was a great lesson. He was not only the leader of India. He was a world leader and there is much for Singaporeans to learn from his teachings, values and life. And that would be the objectives of the Abdul Kalam Vision Society (Singapore)."

The society's first project, undertaken in collaboration with the Singapore Narayana Mission in Yishun, was the donation of wheelchairs for handicapped people. The second project, undertaken on 15 October 2018, was "Keeping Little India Clean and Environmentally-friendly". This was in collaboration with the National Environmental Agency and the Little India Shopkeepers' Association (LISHA).

The project would be in keeping with the implementation of the cooperation between India and Singapore "to achieve the UN Sustainable Development Goal of clean water and sanitation for our people for generations to come."[46]

The third project, carried out in collaboration with Mr Nirmalan Pillay and family as well as the Singapore Indian Association, was to bring cheer to 242 residents of the Sree Narayana Mission on the occasion of the Deepavali celebrations on 4 November 2018.

The AKVS will stay focused on Abdul Khalam's core messages and help to spread them to the world. A forthcoming project would be joining the national effort to fight against diabetes. Wherever inspiration comes from, as it did for me through the AKVS, as long as it is for the benefit of people in need, it should be supported.

---

[46] Op-ed by Prime Minister Lee Hsien Loong, "Singapore and India – A Shared Vision for a Cleaner Future" (*The Straits Times*, 3 October 2018).

CHAPTER 19

Lessons I Learnt from Five Decades of Interaction with the Late Mr SR Nathan

I first met Mr Nathan on 20 April 1968. That date is etched in my memory because it was on that day that I had my first lesson in social service. Since then, I learnt the following lessons from and through him.

Mr Nathan was the chairman of the Seamen's Welfare Board and I was a Ministry of Labour representative on the Board. After a meeting of the Board, and as we were walking back to our respective offices, a distraught-looking seaman approached Mr Nathan. The man said he was facing some work-related problems for which he needed Mr Nathan's help.

Noting it was near lunch time, Mr Nathan asked the man whether he had eaten. When the man replied that he had not, Mr Nathan gave him five dollars and asked him to go and have his lunch. He immediately contacted Mr Choo, the Secretary of the Board, and had the problem resolved. The lesson I learnt from this episode was that the basic needs of a person in distress, in this case hunger, should be dealt with first. Everything else can follow thereafter.

Years later, when I helped to set up a welfare programme in the Singapore Indian Association called "Helping People from falling through the Cracks", the cardinal principle that was adopted was "urgent assistance to solve an immediate problem". Mr Nathan continued to be my mentor in the field of social service from that time onwards.

The second lesson that I learnt was the importance of strengthening the social fabric of Singapore. Mr Nathan maintained that racial harmony and religious tolerance were the building blocks for strengthening the social fabric of Singapore. In an interview with Ms Sithara Doraisamy on 31 October 2015, Mr Nathan elaborated on his views as follows:[47]

> Race is under our skin. The beauty of Singapore is that we are colour blind, we are not Chinese or Malay, or Indian or Eurasian. We are Singaporeans.

Mr Nathan said: "Follow your heart as long as you can and do your part for the well-being of fellow Singaporeans." True to his character, Mr Nathan did not merely preach but put into practice what he believed in. He was a former chairman of the Hindu Endowments Board and the Hindu Advisory Board. He also played a key role in the establishment of SINDA, which has become the umbrella body looking after the educational and social needs of the Indian community. I am privileged to be following in Mr Nathan's footsteps and serving in all three institutions. Upon assuming the presidency, he initiated

[47] Interview published in *Community Leadership Digest* (31 October 2015).

the Community Challenge for the public to make donations. The donations would then be distributed to various organisations.

The third lesson was the need to enhance inter-religious harmony in Singapore. The IRO was close to Mr Nathan's heart. As patron of the organisation, he took a keen interest in its activities. Noting the rise of religious extremism and growing intolerance among faiths, Mr Nathan urged the organisation to reiterate the message of peace and harmony. With his support, I was appointed a member of IRO and subsequently became the president for a year.

The fourth lesson that Mr Nathan taught me was the need to advance and protect Singapore's interests through diplomacy. In August 1972, I moved to the MFA, which was then located in City Hall. From that position, I was able to observe Mr Nathan in action in many situations.

Due to several postings abroad, Indonesia from 1973 to 1976, the Soviet Union from 1979 to 1982, the United Kingdom from 1982 to 1986, and the United Nations (Geneva) from 1991 to 1996, I did not have many opportunities to interact with Mr Nathan in the MFA.

I was, however, at Headquarters when he returned to the MFA as Permanent Secretary, with Mr Chia Cheong Fook as Second Permanent Secretary. This was to be a momentous turning point in the life of the Ministry.

As Mr Nathan puts it in his book, *An Unexpected Journey:*[48]

> My brief was to focus on the internal workings of the organisation and shake it up to improve the quality of the work being done.

Speaking appreciatively of the young MFA diplomats under his charge, Mr Nathan added: "Whatever the issue, the people at Ministry of Foreign Affairs learnt their trade the hard way, in the trenches. There were few books, authorities or precedents to rely on. It was our wits that helped us move forward."

I must add, however, that in non-official social interactions, Mr Nathan was all "sugar and spice". His attachment to family and friends is legendary. The annual Deepavali dinner that he and Mrs Nathan hosted was a high point in the social calendar.

Subsequently, as ambassadors, Mr Nathan and I found ourselves on the frontline dealing with the Michael Fay incident: he as ambassador to the US and I as Singapore's ambassador to WTO. Mr Nathan's role in this saga has been well documented and I have also discussed it earlier in this book. The moral of the story of the Michael Fay incident is, where national interest is concerned, one does not buckle. Mr Nathan did not. Neither did I.

---

[48] SR Nathan with Timothy Auger, *An Unexpected Journey: Path to the Presidency* (Editions Didier Millet, 2011) pp 325–326.

Mr Nathan was dedicated to promoting Singapore. This was my fourth lesson. From him, I learnt the role that diplomacy plays in fostering good relations with the rest of the world. I was able to play host to Mr Nathan in 2003 when he, as Chancellor of the National University of Singapore, led the NUS golf team to play the University of Malaya team, headed by its then Chancellor, Sultan Azlan Shah. This was during a period of tension in bilateral relations when all sporting and other exchanges were curtailed by the Malaysian side, to express the Mahathir government's displeasure towards Singapore over a range of unresolved issues. Both the Chancellors agreed that this long-standing bilateral sporting exchange should not fall victim to political contretemps.

Although a non-golfer, Mr Nathan sportingly rode in the golf buggy and participated in the after-golf dinner celebration. Thanks to this gracious gesture by the two Heads of State in their capacities as Chancellors, this sporting link between the two universities has grown from strength to strength.

The fifth lesson that I learnt was the need to pay continuing attention to the problems of the underclass in society.

After finishing his two-term presidency, Mr Nathan returned to his original passion in public life: social service. He took a special interest in the issue of the growing income inequality that was becoming evident in the socio-economic landscape of the country. Mr Nathan feared that, left unaddressed, this issue would have an adverse impact on the carefully cultivated social fabric of the country.

Another of Mr Nathan's concerns was the position of the underclass, especially those living in one-room HDB flats. He wanted a research study to be undertaken on this issue. Whenever I visited him in hospital, it was apparent that these two concerns were uppermost in his mind. Earlier, he had commissioned a working group, which was chaired by Ambassador B Jayachandran, to look into the social problems affecting the Indian community. I was a member of that working group.

Always on the lookout for opportunities for Indian youths to better themselves, Mr Nathan felt that football was a useful social mechanism to achieve that purpose. Recalling the likes of Sundaramoorthy, Rajagopal and Suriamoorthy, he shared with me his wish to see the current generation of Indian youth represented in the national football team. Rising to the challenge, SINDA has started a football training scheme aimed at nurturing a pool of young players, who can rise up the ranks and strive to play for the national team. SINDA is well-placed to fulfil Mr Nathan's wish.

Reflective of his concerns, Mr Nathan supported the Singapore Indian Association's "Helping People from Falling through the Cracks" programme. Mr Nathan was to be the Guest of Honour for a fundraising lunch on 9 July 2015. That was not to be because shortly before that, he was taken ill and hospitalised. With his demise, a pillar of support was lost, for the country, community and myself.

Mr Nathan's legacy in the field of social work can best be encapsulated by the message he gave to Mr KV Veloo, a fellow social worker and long-time friend:[49]

> He made me realise that as social workers, we were little persons serving a great cause – touching lives, healing rifts, and filling needs. It is a simple principle that has guided my journey as a social worker until today.

Like Mr Veloo, this is the greatest lesson I learnt from a man who rose from humble beginnings to become the "People's President" of Singapore.

---

[49] A Mushahid & R Kumar (eds), *Remembering SR Nathan: A Mentor for All Seasons* (World Scientific, 2017) pp 153–154.

CHAPTER 20

My Journey Continues

Starting the 82nd year of my life, and in reasonably good health, I feel that it is too early to write the concluding chapter to this book. God willing, I might have a few more years to devote to family, friends and society.

Apart from golf that I play with the Gartshore Group (Tan Keng Jin, George Lee, AT Lim, Karmjit Singh, Alan Goh, Choy Moo Chee, Mick Aw, Alfred Ang, Harold Foo, Yeoh Sin Hock, Dicky Goh, Chen, Peck Chong Beng, Robert White, Brian Miles, Ella, Andrew Chow, Lucy, James Fu, Francis, Vincent and Ray), I will also spend some time in supporting the Arts, and Indian classical music and dance in particular. Several years ago, I came into contact with Mr and Mrs Sathyalingam. Coming from Jaffna, Sri Lanka, they started a dance company called Apsaras Arts. Sadly, both have passed away. Along with Dr Ma Swan Hoo, Sowndarya Sukumar and Rhama Sankaran, we are giving as much support as we can to this company, now headed by Aravinth Kumarasamy. With Priyan Thavarajah as the lead dancer, Apsaras Arts has taken their performances to various parts of the world, including the UK, Australia, India, Sri Lanka and Malaysia. In Sri Lanka, we met up with our dear friends the Gunasena family.

Indian High Commissioner Jawed Ashraf has given strong support to this group, including making it possible for Apsaras Arts to be represented at the cultural show in New Delhi in 2018. I continue to support Apsaras Arts as the chairman of the company.

I would always be grateful to my friends, Chandra Das (Non-Resident Ambassador to Sri Lanka) and the retired A*Star Chairman, Lim Chuan Poh, who offered advice and assistance at critical junctures of my life.

In the remainder of this journey, I will be guided by two inspiring messages which have served me as guiding posts.

One is by Mahatma Gandhi: "Be the change that you wish to see, the change to be." Just as Gandhiji brought change to an entire nation, each one of us have within ourselves opportunities to make changes in the world we live in. The second message I live and work by is from Mother Theresa: "We all can't do great things, but we all can do small things with great love."

As poet laureate Rabinath Tagore put it in "Gitanjali" (translated by Nilanjana Sengupta):

> What I have seen
> what I have received
> is beyond comparison.
> Amidst this flowing golden ocean
> there blooms a lotus of a hundred petals,
> I am blessed to have partaken of its nectar.

A Letter from President SR Nathan

S R Nathan
Katong Post Office
PO Box 205
Singapore 914307

20th Feb., 2012

My dear Pang,

Over the last 40 years we have said farewell to each other, many a time, as new assignments & challenges came your way.

When I last approached you in 2002 to take over the leadership of ISEAS, ISEAS was in shambles, with its reputation among scholars at its lowest – no longer what it had been since its founding in 1966.

In the past 10 years you have restored ISEAS' reputation beyond expectation, such that it has the brand name of being the premier research centre on South East Asia, not only in this Region, but beyond. Many a scholar is proud to be associated with it and its work.

As we do another farewell, what can I say, my dear friend – other than to wish you once again well, as you face new challenges that will inevitably come your way. I am sure you will be even more successful whatever tasks you next undertake.

P.T.O

Our friendship has been a very enriching one for me — I hope it has been equally so for you.

I end with a Prayer that you + Padmini be blessed with good health, happiness and even greater success in the next leg of your life.

I remain, as always

Nathan.

Author's Note:

The Scribe's Journey

Have you heard the story of how the great Indian epic, the *Mahabharata*, was written? It is believed that when the sage Vyasa wanted to write the epic, he asked Lord Ganesha to be his scribe. As he started to narrate, Ganesha's feather pen broke unfortunately. In not wanting to interrupt the narration, Ganesha broke off half of his tusk and continued with the transcription.

My journey as a "scribe" of this biography was far less dramatic but the story of Ganesha as a scribe resonates with me in many ways. Like Ganesha, I, too, sat for long hours listening to my "Vyasa", Ambassador Kesavapany (or "Uncle Pany", as I fondly call him), and transcribing images, dialogues and poetry into written form. Like the *Mahabharata*, there were many stories within the story of Kesavapany's journey as an ambassador.

It all began in 2017 when a conversation with Uncle Pany drifted into biographies and, specifically, the not uncontested value of sharing his colourful life as a diplomat. I managed to assure him there would be a ready audience out there to appreciate his entertaining adventures in diplomacy and even benefit from his experiences. When we started work in earnest a few months later, we envisioned we would be done in a span of six months. As he recounted his experiences at various stages of his life, I audio-recorded our conversations and took copious notes. Later, these notes and the transcript of the conversations grew into neat chapters. While I worked on my manuscript, he too worked on his. We then spent the next few months merging his version with mine and filling in the gaps. Thankfully, unlike Ganesha, I did not have to struggle to keep up with the narration. My "Vyasa" was only too happy to oblige when I had questions about the sub-plots that he very patiently narrated, pausing to help me with the spelling of a name or filling in a needed detail of an event or the words of a poem that came out in spontaneous bursts. On the last leg of the journey, we checked the manuscript line by line, with both of us taking turns to read the text aloud to the other. Well, that was the plan at least, but, quite often, even during this last leg, he was adding more and more details.

Uncle Pany's memory is a reservoir of intimate details of events, people and conversations. His memory amazed me the most. Often, I found myself looking up the year of an event or the spelling of a prominent member of the community, only to find out that Uncle Pany had got it right. The icing on the cake was hearing him recite poetry, word for word without missing a beat. Some of the poems that are encapsulated in his memories are captured in this book verbatim.

I found myself lost in the English countryside and ballroom dancing, in a time before Malaysia got her independence when he was still a starry-eyed young man, and in the intricacies of foreign diplomacy in different lands.

My journey documenting his life was greatly supported by his wife, Mrs Padmini Kesavapany, who was always within earshot to give us a helping hand. Often, her words would find their way into the book as well. This book would certainly not have been possible without her support. Aunty Padmini, their sons, Murali and Sashi, as well as their grandchildren, Kishan and Jaynna, helped us to select the photographs in this book. The photographs brought more memories flooding back to the family and their anecdotes were later included, which enriched the biography. These anecdotes provide an additional lens on Uncle Pany's life.

I am deeply grateful to Uncle Pany and his family for letting me view their lives with a pair of writer's binoculars. At the end of the day, this is the story of a man who was once told that the birthmark in the shape of a "chakra wheel" on his foot would take him across the oceans many times. It is the story of a man who was inspired by Mr Lee Kuan Yew's speech that he had heard as a young man, motivating him to move to Singapore later and devote his life to the civil service. It is also an ongoing story of a man who never retired, which I know only too well, as I had to struggle to find space in his packed schedule of meetings, charity work and community work to write this story. Something tells me that there is a second volume to this book in the near future. After all, right up to the day we had to hand over the manuscript, he had more to add.

The journey continues.

Dr Anitha Devi Pillai
1 January 2019

My Soul Has A Hat

I counted my years
& realized that I have
Less time to live by,
Than I have lived so far.

I feel like a child who won a pack of candies: at first he ate them with pleasure
But when he realized that there was little left, he began to taste them intensely.

I have no time for endless meetings
where the statutes, rules, procedures & internal regulations are discussed,
knowing that nothing will be done.

I no longer have the patience
To stand absurd people who,
despite their chronological age,
have not grown up.

My time is too short:
I want the essence,
my spirit is in a hurry.
I do not have much candy
In the package anymore.

I want to live next to humans,
very realistic people who know
How to laugh at their mistakes,
Who are not inflated by their own triumphs
& who take responsibility for their actions.
In this way, human dignity is defended
and we live in truth and honesty.

It is the essentials that make life useful.
I want to surround myself with people
who know how to touch the hearts of those whom hard strokes of life
have learned to grow with sweet touches of the soul.

Yes, I'm in a hurry.
I'm in a hurry to live with the intensity that only maturity can give.
I do not intend to waste any of the remaining desserts.

I am sure they will be exquisite,
much more than those eaten so far.
My goal is to reach the end satisfied
and at peace with my loved ones and my conscience.

We have two lives
& the second begins when you realize you only have one.

Mario de Andrade,
San Paolo 1893–1945

About the Authors

K Kesavapany was Singapore's High Commissioner to Malaysia from 1997 to 2002. He served as Singapore's Permanent Representative to the UN in Geneva and was concurrently accredited as Ambassador to Italy and Turkey (1991–1997). He was elected as the first Chairman of the General Council of the WTO when it was established in January 1995. He was also Singapore's Non-Resident Ambassador to the Hashemite Kingdom of Jordan. From 2002 to 2012, he was the Director of the Institute of Southeast Asian Studies, Singapore.

Over the years, he held several prominent portfolios in the social scene of Singapore, including serving as the President of the Singapore Indian Association, President of the Inter-Religious Organization Council, President of Rotary Club of Raffles City, Term Trustee of SINDA, Board Member of the Hindu Endowment Board, as well as a Governor on the Board of the Singapore International Foundation.

Mr Kesavapany is currently an adjunct professor at the Lee Kuan Yew School of Public Policy (National University of Singapore), an executive committee member of the Dyslexia Association of Singapore and the Indian Community Oral History Committee (ICOHC), as well as the President of the Abdul Kalam Vision Society.

Anitha Devi Pillai (Ph.D.) is an applied linguist and a teacher educator. She lectures pre-service and in-service English Language teachers at the National Institute of Education (Nanyang Technological University, Singapore). Her teaching modules focus on writing skills and writing pedagogy.

She was the recipient of the Singapore University of Social Sciences Teaching Merit Award in 2013 and 2014, as well as the Research Excellence Award from *Pravasi Express* in 2017 for her research on the Singapore Malayalee community. In 2019, she was awarded the *Excellence in Teaching Commendation Award 2018* from the National Institute of Education, Nanyang Technological University.

Anitha is the first author of *From Kerala to Singapore: Voices from the Singapore Malayalee Community* (Marshall Cavendish Editions, 2017) and *Project Work: Exploring Processes, Practices and Strategies* (Pearson Education, 2008). She has also published in academic journals and books based on empirical research on writing pedagogy and writing processes as well as poetry and short stories in local and international journals.

"It was such a treat for me to read *From Estate to Embassy: Memories of an Ambassador* by K Kesavapany with Anitha Devi Pillai.

It flowed so seamlessly that I read it in one sitting without any break.

Ambassador Pany is such a lovable people person that it is no surprise at all to read about how he has networked so smoothly through all aspects of his life from career to charity and from politics to poetry.

I propose an addition to the title *From Estate to Embassy: From Excellence to Ecstasy*. I mean ecstasy to include Pany's spiritual side as well with his interfaith journey.

My second proposal is that Pany may wish to say more or highlight chapter 13, "Returning to my Roots". I recall that when Mr Lee Kuan Yew spoke to us in Kuala Lumpur on his last sentimental journey to Malaysia, his speech was peppered with one recurring phrase, "as Pany told me". It is an awesome feat for any mortal to make such an impact on a leader as formidable as Mr Lee.

My second proposal is therefore both for idealistic and practical reasons."

Dato' Dr M Shanmughalingam

author of *Marriage and Mutton Curry* (best seller)

"Reading about Kesavapany's personal recollections, one can better understand Singapore's historical journey and the role he and his peers have played leading up to what we know today.

True to form, his detailed descriptions of his friends reflect his character of being ever grateful for even the smallest deed extended to him. To his friends and his adopted country, he is extremely loyal to a fault!

This book serves to remind the younger generations of the existential fact of Singapore life and its inherited vulnerabilities and the ever relevant human values required to deal with these issues."

Ambassador Zulkifli Baharudin

"Publishing is an art my good friend Pany excels in. During his days with ISEAS, he would have released a book every couple of weeks – a feat not many can achieve. No wonder his biography *Estate to Embassy* adopts a simple, elegant and easy to read (journalistic) style, encouraging even a non-serious, casual reader like me to read the manuscript from end to end!

Pany, the quiet but successful 'diplomat' with an illustrious career full of measurable outcomes (his stint with WTO, for example) also had the time and mindset to focus on other interests as well, outside of official work (to balance work with life). Recognition and awards granted to him by many governments and multilateral institutions are not really a surprise to those who know him well.

But what strikes me the most about Pany is his unassuming nature and friendly demeanour. Always caring for the challenged, his concern and readiness to do more than 'something' by way of tangible, timely help for those in need, are qualities not seen in many. His involvements with IA (particularly the "Falling through the crack" initiative), HEB/HAB, IHC, SINDA, IRO and a few others amply validate his genuine interest in the service of community far beyond the call of duty."

Ambassador R Jayachandran
Chairman, Hindu Endowment Board

"*From Estate to Embassy* is not just a biography. It's our history presented through his story. It's a story about finding joy in circumstance, about self-belief and passion, and the need for compassion. The emotions are real. Pany, with your famous smile coming through the words, you have reminded me of the importance of making time for people, and being grateful. Thank you, my friend!"

Viswa Sadasivan
former Nominated Member of Parliament, Singapore

"It is said that a journey is best measured in friends not in miles', as is my journey of friendship of near 60 years with the Pany family. It is one of my cherished treasures that I often recall, relive and bask in. Memories of the times that our families had spent together in Haig Road and the East Coast as Pany moved from 'estate to diplomat' brought a smile to my face.

The foundation of our friendship was a love for the performing arts, the community and the family. We shared laughter, joyful moments, troubled times, long chats. Your family was there for me and my children when I lost Rajan in 1977 and then my father in 1982, and gave us unwavering affection, care and concern.

As you moved from 'estate to diplomat', we were separated physically but had no problem picking up the threads of our friendship when you returned even for a short period. The bond that I share with your family is extremely special, strong and unusual. We have no expectations from each other and we have never hesitated to ask each other for any help. Friends like you are hard to find, difficult to let go, and difficult to forget.

Thank you for being there, Pany and Pappi!"

Dr Uma Rajan BBM, PBM, PBS
Consultant (Student & Elder Care) & Indian Arts, Culture & Heritage

---

"Ambassador Kesavapany's autobiography is not an ego-trip for the author. It is a revelation of a man who is humble, kind and truly grateful for the many blessings he has received. It is also a heterobiography about many who touched his life and he is quick to credit them for many of his achievements in one lifetime. Recollected with historical accuracy, recounted with diplomacy and related with authenticity, his life and work continue to inspire me."

Dr William Wan (JP)
General Secretary, Singapore Kindness Movement

"*From Estate to Embassy* is not the story of a man with vaulting ambitions who is self-absorbed in wanting to reach the pinnacle. It is the story of a gentle, humane person who recounts his experiences handling a variety of tasks which he had not sought but had landed on his plate, which nevertheless he executes with great skill. The concern he shows for his pet dog Benji as well as any human being who needs help reveals the character of the man. The book is an easy read, giving interesting insights from 1967 when Pany gets that letter from Singapore."

Ambassador Gopinath Pillai

"K Kesavapany is a man of many talents who had a distinguished career in the Singapore civil service, especially in the field of diplomacy and foreign relations.

He has won many distinguished awards from so many countries for his contributions.

I came to know him when he was Singapore's High Commissioner to Malaysia. He used to engage me on some matters and it was he who introduced me to Minister Mentor Lee Kuan Yew during one of his visits to Malaysia in the late 1990s.

Following retirement from UKM, I joined ISEAS as a Senior Research Fellow at the time Kesavapany was the director.

During my brief stay in ISEAS, I had the opportunity to work closely with him on projects related to early Indian influence and on the Chola voyages.

Kesavapany might have been a civil servant but he was one of the best directors ISEAS had. His broad knowledge of history enabled him to commission outstanding works at ISEAS. I am proud to have been involved in some of the projects at ISEAS.

Kesavapany might have sought a formal retirement from the civil service, but his role in society seems unceasing. He has taken a lead in rendering social service to the needy and occasionally speaking on matters of spiritualism."

Professor Ramasamy Palanisamy

Deputy Chief Minister of the State of Penang, Malaysia